C000005795

And then there was  Maggie

And Then There Was Maggie

Keith Weaver

IGUANA

Copyright © 2022 Keith Weaver
Published by Iguana Books
720 Bathurst Street, Suite 303
Toronto, ON M5S 2R4

All rights reserved. No part of this publication may be reproduced, stored
in a retrieval system or transmitted, in any form or by any means, electronic,
mechanical, recording or otherwise (except brief passages for purposes of
review) without the prior permission of the author.

Publisher: Meghan Behse
Editor: Paula Chiarcos
Front cover design: Victoria Feistner

ISBN 978-1-77180-596-4 (paperback)
ISBN 978-1-77180-595-7 (epub)

This is an original print edition of *And Then There Was Maggie.*

DEDICATION

To the memory of my unforgettable wife and life partner, Margaret Ruth Weaver (Maggie), an extraordinary woman it was my good fortune to meet and marry. Maggie was my soulmate in many ways, and she changed my life fundamentally.

With my deepest love, Maggie, for who you were, for our wonderful life together, for what you will always mean to me, and for how you inspired so many people.

PREFACE

This book is a statement of profound gratitude for the woman who shared her life with me, my wife, Maggie. Maggie died on January 12, 2022, at the far-too-young age of seventy-one. Maggie and I had been married for almost forty-nine years, and I had known her for fifty-two years. Our life together was rich and full, a fantastic journey.

Writing this book has been one way of coming to terms with an immense loss. Too much focus on loss can drag one down, and I wanted these words to turn away from thoughts of loss, to the extent one can do that, and to speak instead of the great gift and the soaring power that our life together delivered. I wanted the story to be principally about Maggie. But since our lives were so interlocked over such a long period, and since it's me doing the writing, the story inevitably must involve my perspective. Although I have tried to limit the intrusion of my persona into the story, I haven't been as successful at that as I had hoped.

Many people who knew Maggie were devastated by the news of her death and were overcome when I told them I was writing this book. They all insisted that they should receive copies. And that has been done.

Beyond that group of friends and colleagues, large as it is, there might be little interest in what I have set down here. But I hope this account can serve as a representative statement that there are many happy and fulfilling marriages out there.

CHAPTER 1

WHO WAS MAGGIE?

From Boars Hill one can look out over the flood plain of the Thames and the Cherwell. On an early morning in summer, if you are lucky, the sun will begin its task of burning off the thick duvet of mist that has settled on the flood plain overnight. Spikes will begin to protrude as the duvet thins. Soon the spikes will become spires and will glow golden in the early light. These are the dreaming spires that Matthew Arnold made famous in his poem "Thyrsis".

And the city is Oxford.

Maggie Walker was born in Oxford on February 24, 1950, at John Radcliffe Hospital. She emerged about twenty minutes after her twin brother, Chris. Maggie and Chris were taken from the hospital to go home — "home" was a housing estate near the nuclear research establishment at Harwell, south of Oxford. More specifically, home at Harwell was initially at 25 Wayland Crescent, and later was at 7 Severn Road. These dwellings were part of a group of prefabs built for workers at the research site. Maggie spent her first six years in Wayland Crescent.

Through her parents, Maggie had connections to other locations in the north and the southwest of England.

Maggie's mother was born Joan Irwin on June 26, 1924, in Bristol where she was raised. Bristol is awash in history, having been a major port for exploration and for trade between England and the rest of the world. It was from Bristol that John Cabot set out in 1497. The great engineer I. K. Brunel is linked to Bristol through the SS *Great Britain*, the world's first iron-hull ship, which is docked permanently there, and through the nearby Clifton Suspension Bridge which he designed and built. Also in Bristol is the Llandoger Trow, a well-known old pub where Daniel Defoe is reported to have got the inspiration for *Robinson Crusoe* from Alexander Selkirk. The Llandoger Trow is also associated with Long John Silver in Robert Louis Stevenson's *Treasure Island*. Maggie related all this lore to me, eager to share her rich diet of history and culture. Maggie's Uncle Alec was a long-time resident of Bristol and knew all its stories.

To the north in England is the gorgeous city of York, and to the east of it, the seaside town of Scarborough. Maggie's father, John Walker, was born in York on September 25, 1923, and was raised in Scarborough. John was an only child and his father died when he was quite young. Maggie and I visited Scarborough many times, a place that she and her brother had travelled to in their youth. Maggie's grandmother and a delightful family friend, Bertha, lived there until they both died in the 1980s. As a girl, Maggie loved to do wave-dodging, watching waves crash in from the North Sea and trying not to be soaked, something that had been a source of great excitement for her. There was also the ritual of buying freshly dressed crab from vendors on the foreshore.

In the nineteenth and early twentieth centuries, Scarborough was a summer destination for reasonably well-off people from industrial areas, such as Sheffield. Our visits there, Maggie's and mine when we lived in London, were by train, and I remember clearly the announcement that we had arrived on the coast, the announcement being the cries of dozens and perhaps hundreds of gulls we heard the moment we stepped off the train. To the north of Scarborough is the lovely hamlet of Robin Hood's Bay. Local enthusiasm for Robin Hood's activities in the region is not dampened in the least by the lack of any real proof that Robin Hood ever existed or that he had overwhelmed French pirates and distributed their loot among residents of the village. Somewhat farther north of Scarborough is the town of Whitby, birthplace of James Cook, whose name still appears in the local church. Maggie needed no encouragement to revisit any of these places.

Maggie's parents were both accomplished. Joan received a degree in mathematics from the University of London (Westfield College), which was evacuated to St. Peter's Hall in Oxford during the Second World War. John graduated from Cambridge as an electrical engineer. Joan and John were both intellectually energetic; they had wide interests, were well read, were equal to any conversational situation, and could bring any party to life. Joan was an excellent cook, among many other things, and John was a keen pianist, also among many other things. Although I was a Johnny-come-lately on the scene, I found the Walker household to be one of music, discussion, argument, laughter, and clever wordplay, and I have no reason to think that it was ever anything other than that.

But long before I arrived on the scene, there were Maggie's childhood years. In the 1950s, Oxford and the countryside south of Oxford were far different places than they are today. Although the years immediately after World War II were difficult in England, young children noticed only some aspects of this, if they noticed anything at all. Rationing was in place, and that might have been difficult for anyone to ignore. Families had to make every penny count, and Maggie recalled noticing her mother going through the pockets of coats and jackets looking for loose change. There was school to attend, however, and children will always find ways to play.

Maggie and Chris attended the primary school at Harwell, but they were quite a handful since they were always bickering. The teachers got round that problem by placing one of them in the next higher class. That one was Maggie. I'm quite sure that these arrangements didn't go unnoticed by Maggie's parents. Each in his or her own way, the members of Maggie's family were achievers. Living at Harwell meant that they were close to what was an important technical effort, the beginnings of the peaceful applications of nuclear energy. And I often had the feeling from things Maggie said that even as a young girl she was aware that her parents' work was important.

At Harwell, John was part of the team that designed and built the first nuclear reactor in Britain. That reactor was called BEPO (British

Experimental Pile; the "O" being added for reasons that never were clear to me). At about the same time, Joan was part of a group who were doing lattice calculations. By hand. "Lattice" refers to the arrangement (geometric pattern and spacing) of fuel channels or fuel rods in a reactor core. The ideal lattice places each fuel channel at a separation from its neighbours that results in a sustainable and controllable chain reaction. Nobody at Harwell knew what the ideal lattice was because BEPO was a reactor first. It had never been done before in Britain or in Europe. Finding the characteristics of this ideal lattice was then a matter of trial and error, and many different possible lattices had to be postulated and a tedious and complex hand calculation done for each possibility to see which lattice gave the desired result. This was all highly secret stuff, and the people involved were bound to silence about their work for many years. But this was in the immediate post-war years, and although times were still hard, the future looked better, and to work in the emerging field of "nuclear energy" was something very heady.

It was against this background that Maggie spent her early years.

The nuclear business was an exotic one in those days, and the people working in it had to be inventive in developing a unique new energy source while responding to the demands of the taxing technologies that would enable it. Those people developed skills and mastered techniques that were well ahead of the curve and highly desired elsewhere, and it was John's work in the nuclear business that eventually resulted in him moving from Harwell to work for Sperry. This involved a family move, and the Walker family soon was established in an area of Stroud known as Cainscross, although John had a longish commute from there to his work.

At Cainscross, Maggie and her family lived in a house named Braybrooke. I never did visit Braybrooke, but it was from there that Maggie attended Stroud High School for Girls. Maggie never had a problem with school, and from what I know of this period in her life, she excelled academically and enjoyed relatively effortless scholastic achievement. She also engaged in sports, and she often spoke later about field hockey, something that appears to have meant a good deal to her as a girl. Maggie also played tennis, her father having been a fairly accomplished tennis player. I remember seeing the worn patch on her tennis racket cover where she said it rubbed against the wheel of her bicycle as she rode to and from school.

It seems as well that Maggie's name was linked to certain "events". One such "event" she told me about was having to explain how a pair of her knickers had managed to be hoisted to the top of the school flagpole. It was clear that they were Maggie's knickers. Everyone's clothes had to have their owner's name appear in them so that clothes and girls could be reliably reunited after sports classes. I don't know whether an explanation for the hoisted knickers ever emerged.

During these years of Maggie's childhood and early adolescence, the family fortunes became more comfortable as John's career advanced. John was to change employers again, this time moving to Xerox. That coincided approximately with another family move — a short distance from Cainscross to the nearby village of Westrip, which is also in the Stroud valleys. In Westrip the family occupied a lovely cottage called Sandpipers, which was located in Sandpits Lane.

Each stage in John's employment brought him into contact with many people, colleagues and supervisors, a few of whom appeared later in Maggie's life. More on all that later.

Throughout John's working life, he was associated with the Masons and he rose to high levels in that organization. This figured prominently in a late stage of his life.

During all this time, Maggie's mother, Joan, most definitely did not shrink as a violet or as any other example of flora or fauna. Joan was a forthright and forceful woman, someone who Maggie always admired and who served as a model, some aspects of which Maggie followed as she built her own life and approach to the world. Joan was a mathematics teacher for quite a few years, and when she gave up teaching she became a driving force in the local Townswomen's Guild.

Joan and John were also keen gardeners in their distinct ways. They both could identify a wide range of plants, whether tame or wild. Sandpipers consisted of three eighteenth-century farm workers' cottages that had been knocked together to form a long narrow house, long before the Walkers took up residence. Sandpipers was the last of a series of houses along one side of Sandpits Lane, which ran up a fairly steep hill from Westrip and eventually crested that hill and petered out to a track. Standing in Sandpits Lane and looking over a dry-stone wall into the front garden at Sandpipers, one regarded the long front side of the house. The rear of the house backed onto the face of an old quarry. Immediately in front of the house was a rectangular lawn, which was bounded on three sides by a lovely floral border, the border on the right-hand side being the most elaborate. A path led along the left-hand side of the lawn to the door that served as the main entrance to the house and opened into the kitchen. Near the kitchen door was a small herb garden and a rockery. A vegetable garden climbed the hillside behind the rockery.

Joan took good care of her floral border and made sure that something was happening in it in every season. She would spend considerable time making sure that her plants did well by moving them around, replacing them, or just pulling them up and examining them. And the floral border was an essential part of a "tour" any visitor to Sandpipers was taken on. John worked the vegetable garden, and it yielded most things one would expect to find in an English vegetable garden: peas, runner beans, broad beans, carrots, parsnips, and various greens.

Outside the kitchen door hung a cast-iron triangle, and Joan would often ring this triangle at 11:00 a.m., signalling a coffee break called "elevenses" for those working outside. After I had been accepted on the scene, I would steal one or two pieces of flapjack at elevenses from a large glass jar just inside the kitchen. It soon became apparent that Joan was an active part of this theft conspiracy, since the flapjack jar was always full.

I came to understand what, for Maggie, was a many-sided meaning to the idea of "home". England was home for her. Her several childhood residences were home. Sandpipers, as I came to know it, was very much home. These were distinct from my very different personal origins. In the rest of this story, the idea "home" surfaces many times. But in a very real sense, Maggie was essential to what became my own idea of home.

There is a lot more to tell here that would give additional colour, shape, and depth to Maggie's life, and some of it will appear later. At this point I want to describe the path by which Maggie collected me.

❧

Chapter 2

MEETING MAGGIE

Over all the years I was with Maggie, I cannot remember a time when I wasn't aware of her smile.

It seems that it was always there. And it seemed to arise from many sources.

Sometimes it was an outward hint of some private personal enjoyment.

Sometimes it appeared because of a glimmer of humour recognized, a pun deciphered, a double meaning unveiled, a situation unexpectedly interpreted, a rich ore vein of possibility suddenly discovered, a cultured moment savoured, or just an expression of pure joy.

Sometimes it was an invitation.

Sometimes it was a message that existed beyond words and was transmitted across a pillow, across a dining table set for two, across a room.

And sometimes, quite often in fact, it was a great beacon of life being lived in the instant — of friendship here, now, and ever, of deciding to cut loose for just a moment, of some inspired bit of whimsy, of an arresting wisp of humour about to be set free, of professional camaraderie, of collective achievement, of group bonding.

Maggie's brilliant smile and her beaming face were known and recognized, it seems, by everyone. That smile and the face radiating life were just two of the engaging features that came as part of the package known as Maggie.

I basked in the glow of that smile for fifty-two years.

Everyone who knew Maggie knew that she was a great fountain of friendship, of general knowledge, of curiosity, of eagerness to help others, of tremendous commitment, and of unquenchable desire to live the moment with others.

But back in 1970, Maggie, her smile, and everything else associated with her were in my then unknown future.

In the pages that follow, I will try to paint a picture of Maggie as I knew her and as others knew her. This account will skip around somewhat, but I will start it by relating details on how Maggie and I met.

During my third year in chemical engineering at the University of Toronto, I began pondering, in my then gormless way, where my life was headed. I hope that I'm a bit less gormless now, that I have reaped some gorm during the intervening decades. In my early twenties and having no informed vision of the world and no idea of what my place in it might be, I simply thrashed around for a while, looking for a direction. Somehow, I came across an organization called IAESTE, the International Association for the Exchange of Students for Technical Experience. For most university students back then, and remember that this was 1970, the earnings from a summer job were needed to pay for the next year's study, and those jobs often involved doing some unappealing work. Here was a chance to try for a position somewhere in Europe. But of course this wasn't just Europe, it was **EUROPE**!!

So I applied to IAESTE, practically starved myself for more than half a year to finance this caper, and tried to ignore any negative impacts. The arrangements were made quickly, but it all seemed well off in the future. So it was in a state of some dismay that a jet-lagged and slightly disoriented student stumbled off the bus at the Victoria Air Terminal in London on a sunny morning, sometime in early May of 1970.

I had a plan, of sorts. My IAESTE work term was for eight weeks in July and August at the Atomic Energy Research Establishment (AERE) located near the village of Harwell in what was then sleepy Berkshire countryside south of Oxford. For the rest of May and June, I was going to see as much of continental Europe as possible. I had a first-class Eurail pass good for two months. It all seemed satisfactorily practical and utilitarian, even though I was somehow aware, in a hazy youthful way, that I was headed for as much unstructured excitement as possible. I was on my way to Europe, a place full of old buildings and free spirits. But in the meantime, I would spend a few days in London.

It took only a few hours in the great English capital for me to begin to grasp just what it was that I had embarked upon. Mawkish Disney images of London were quickly torn from my worldview, uprooted, and burned. What I found around me was something having a depth that Disney could never capture: a city that embodied history, that showed faces both elegant and brutal, and that displayed an essence I couldn't pinpoint at first but came to recognize later — a multi-layered and multi-dimensional accretion of living culture.

But let's skip past all this. It will come back later.

I did my tour of Europe, made full use of the Eurail pass by travelling well over five thousand kilometres. This wasn't just an exercise in racking up distance. There was an objective — to see as much of Europe as I could, if only on a fleeting basis, and to determine which parts of it I would like to revisit in future. It was indeed a cunning plan, but it didn't work. I found that I wanted to go back to every country I visited.

So on the appointed day in July, I presented myself at the administration building at AERE Harwell (and I will refer to the site as just "Harwell" from here on) to be signed on for my eight-week student-work period. There was a good deal of paperwork, including the requirement to sign the Official Secrets Act (an oddly perverse hope that I was delighted to have realized), and then, along with about fifteen other students, I was bussed to Oxford where I had been assigned digs in Walton Crescent, just off Walton Street. Three days later, on Monday morning, I boarded the bus that would take me and the other students to Harwell for our first day at work. The work was interesting, and the people in the group where I worked were very interesting, but an event took place the following Monday, an event that turned out to be important.

I boarded the bus to Harwell on my second Monday. The bus threaded its way through Oxford, picking up other students at a handful of locations. At the last stop, on The High not far from Magdalen Bridge, a small clutch of students boarded. One of these students was smiling and laughing, wore a midlength pale-blue summer jacket with darker-blue vertical stripes, had hair short at back and sides and off the face to show a high forehead, and whose features were strong enough to have tremendous appeal. I was surprised by it then, and I can still recall the strength of my response at clapping eyes on a complete stranger.

That was my first sight of Maggie. I didn't know it then, but looking back much later, it was obvious enough to me that I had been hooked from the get-go. Instantly. Over the course of a few days, I got to know her name, and on the Friday of that week I learned a bit more when we queued at noon to collect our weekly pocket money of £5 15s. Maggie's maiden name was Walker, so she was immediately in front of me in this "dole" queue. We had an interesting exchange on that particular occasion. Maggie was always forthright, but that characteristic was more pronounced when she was younger.

"Nice jacket", she said, the look in her eye indicating something less than a full compliment, her words more a challenging opening gambit than a conversation stopper. I was wearing my blue leather U of T engineering jacket, and it became obvious to me quickly enough that many people I encountered considered my jacket to be decidedly "un-English". But it made me look like I had eighteen-inch biceps, so any smiles from young men tended to be friendly.

"Poverty's child has to take what he can get", I said and shrugged in a way that I hoped was self-deprecating.

"Rubbish!" she replied, through a smile that precluded offence. "Looks like real leather."

This sort of banter continued until we reached the cash desk, and a woman who apparently was trained never to smile handed us our weekly dole curtly.

"She looks like somebody from *Oliver Twist*", Maggie offered as we moved away. We bought sandwiches in the cafeteria then ate them sitting on a bench next to the tennis courts. From Maggie's seemingly inexhaustible store of general knowledge, I learned about the plague of tiny flying insects known in that part of the world as "thunder bugs". Maggie told me that they really were thrips.

"There's no singular", she added, and I was left to puzzle over that one.

Thus began my introduction to a strong-minded, well-informed, but personable young woman.

For my project at Harwell, I was assigned to a group associated with the research reactor named Pluto, and it took no time at all to fall into a working routine with that group. They were all amiable, technically sound, and well informed on many nontechnical topics, something that I quickly recognized was common to many educated English people. If it sounds like I was surprised at this, that's because I was. I had come from a background where the possession of a good general knowledge was somewhere between uncommon and unknown but closer to the unknown end. It took little time for me to begin asking myself why I found this characteristic so engaging.

One of the people in my work group was about my age, and he and I went for the occasional pint. The man who headed the group was an impish Irishman who seemed to have a rock-solid grasp of just about every technical subject. Another member of the group, a soft-spoken gentleman who lived in Abingdon, was twenty-five years my senior and a self-taught expert in almost every aspect of statistics. That interest rubbed off on me and it remains strong more than fifty years later. I joined in the daily darts game at lunchtime, and they were all forgiving of my low skill level, well below rank amateur.

I had a specific project, and I worked away at it. During the second week of work, I needed several technical references, and I got directions on how to find the library. The library was outside the higher-security area, and there was a ritual for leaving that area and returning to it. In the library I immediately came across the young woman, Maggie, who had been in front of me in the dole queue and who I learned was spending her student work time as the most junior level of library assistant. A casual hello and smiles of recognition led to a brief discussion and an arrangement to meet that evening in a pub in Oxford then known as The Golden Cross Inn in Cornmarket. With Maggie's help, I found the books and papers I needed. Helping me find those references seemed to make Maggie curious about my work colleagues, and she did meet some of them eventually.

Of the fifteen or so students billeted in Oxford, for some reason I came to know only one of them, apart from Maggie, reasonably well. I believe I was the only student not from Britain and I recall feeling somewhat inhibited because of that. And not without reason. On almost every aspect of England and English life, I knew little or nothing and I had no desire to have my ignorance put into stark relief. The one student I came to know, Robert, had digs in the same house as me in Walton Crescent. He was a Scot studying at Heriot-Watt University and seemed to consider himself also something of an outsider in Oxford. Emboldened by our common alien status, we explored Oxford together, talked about where we came from, and shared many takeout curries and Chinese meals. But he had the advantage over me since he knew bits and pieces about the city and the university. As we walked by the Sheldonian Theatre during my first week in Oxford, he pointed to the carved stone heads on pillars surrounding the theatre. They were badly corroded and disfigured due to air pollution. To me they looked like either the faces of lepers or men utterly disgusted at something. The latter image was closer to the accepted local description, he said, which was that of someone smelling shit for the first time.

Okay.

Maggie and I continued to get together at irregular intervals. From occasional pub evenings to impromptu sandwich lunches as we walked around part of the Harwell site, I got to know more about her. At that point, the time I spent with Maggie was nothing more than an interesting connection to someone whose background was well outside my experience. I learned later from Maggie that during those weeks she was indulging something like the same curiosity at something like the same level.

The eight weeks passed quickly. I did a good deal of Oxford exploration on my own. Robert and I roamed the streets on occasion in the evening. But I found that I was doing more and more exploring with Maggie. I got to know the pubs reasonably well. Maggie introduced me to the Martyrs' Memorial, we visited the Ashmolean Museum and the Pitt Rivers Museum, and I headed to the public library quite often doing catch-up on local history. The Lamb and Flag pub was not far from my digs, and Maggie and I visited often. I came to know the literary history, mostly from Maggie, associated with another pub, The Eagle and Child. The White Horse in Broad Street, an air-force pub during the Second World War, became a favourite, long before

Inspector Morse made it known around the world. I remember The White Horse particularly from the first visit Maggie and I made there. An avuncular barman smiled at us.

"Nine!" he said to the room in general. Maggie's smile beamed. I had no idea what he meant. But I learned later that I was the ninth young man who had accompanied Maggie to that particular hostelry.

Another pub Maggie introduced me to was The Turl. I probably visited this one most, partly because of its obscure location, partly because it was such an unconventional watering hole once the entrance was located, and partly because of the mynah bird that sat on a perch just inside the door. That bird had a piercing wolf whistle and in response to a conversational gambit would offer the one-line rejoinder, "Do have a cigar."

Maggie and I also walked to Godstow Lock one Saturday with a picnic lunch, where I learned the hard way that leaning into a gorse bush isn't a good plan. We walked through the University Parks more than once, me not realizing then how significant that location would be. Punting looked to be beyond my competence so I never did offer to treat Maggie to that. Maggie introduced me to the writing of Edmund Crispin and we went to see where *The Moving Toyshop* could have been. I learned that the house where I had digs was on the edge of a region of Oxford known as Jericho, and I spent several days walking all the streets of Jericho, a place made more alluring by the fact that nobody, not even Maggie, seemed able to explain how its name had arisen. One memorable evening, Maggie and I went to an open-air party (it might be called a rave today) in a farmer's field near Kidlington. There was finger food, plenty of beer, loud music, and several hundred young people. The mix of alcohol, music, and the laughter of young people — these all made for a relaxed evening without cares. An impromptu game of football broke out, the football being a head of cabbage someone had found. But the disintegration of the cabbage made the game a short-lived one. It wasn't easy moving around on grass, but as young people we were adaptable. That night was my first time dancing with Maggie and it was a different experience. There was a good deal of stumbling over tufts of grass, each of us grabbing the other to avoid falling down, all of it accompanied by giggling and laughing. Being close to the body of a twenty-year-old young woman wasn't something new to me, but I do recall the novelty of the young woman being English, the dance floor being a pasture, and the surroundings being stone walls and a venerable stone barn.

It was well beyond midnight as we walked home, down Banbury Road, hoping to burn off and exhale some of the alcohol, past some riotous displays of night-flowering nicotiana waving their large flowers at us, past several pubs, well known but now closed and dark, past the Martyrs' Memorial, on to Carfax, and then along The High as I walked Maggie to her digs even though she said it wasn't necessary. I made it back to Walton Crescent but found that the walk home hadn't quite done the job assigned to it since I had to put one foot flat on the floor to prevent the bed from doing end-to-end flips.

My work term drew to a close. I wrote a project report and felt that its slender substance confirmed my feeling I hadn't really achieved all that much. However, my supervisor said it was fine, that they could take advantage of the results I reported. I had farewell drinks with my work colleagues. Robert and I enjoyed one final curry and a bit too much lager. Maggie had started her student term a week later than me, so I was wrapping up ahead of her. She asked me what my plans were when I left Oxford. There was a cousin in Harrow I wanted to spend some time with. A friend was passing through London on his way back to Toronto and we had agreed to have a nice meal in London then rent a car for a few days.

Maggie asked if I would like to visit her family's place in Stroud.

Of course I would.

In Oxford, Maggie and I had a farewell meal at The Horse and Jockey, where I threw financial caution to the wind and ran up a tab of £2 18s. I walked Maggie to her digs for the last time, and the next morning I caught the train to London. There I met my friend Bill. We had a terrific meal in Half Moon Street at a restaurant called Clowns, a spot where Maggie and I would eat several times later, then we rented a car and went off to see a few places Bill wanted to tick off his list.

I had directions to get to Maggie's parents' place in the village of Westrip, which is located on the western slope of the Five Valleys centred on Stroud. Bill and I found Maggie's home with some difficulty, arriving late in the morning. Maggie's parents were completely charming, and we sat in the garden enjoying a drink and wide-ranging conversation, and Bill and I were invited to stay for lunch. It was all very enjoyable. Maggie and I talked quite a bit about Stroud, about Harwell, about Gloucestershire, about what she wanted to do after she finished her studies the following year at Exeter. I was still almost completely gormless at that point, so I likely missed many fine points. But I've looked at pictures from that time and I'm always struck at how youthful and vivacious Maggie looked, something she retained throughout her life. I remember her clearly from that day, and although she really was a bundle of youth, she was also mature beyond her twenty years in many ways.

Maggie showed me through her parents' home. Even then, I still hadn't got used to the idea that many buildings in England display venerable age. As a dwelling, Maggie's parents' home was something beyond my experience but it did speak to me. This was my first visit to a real English country cottage, and I think it was from that point I realized how limited and impoverished were my notions of "living space".

After lunch, we spent another hour in the garden, since it was a lovely warm day. After extended farewells, Bill and I got back in the rental car and drove off. I remember my mixed feelings as we coasted down Sandpits Lane. My sense was still that it had all been a one-time adventure that was now finishing, but something in me wanted it to continue just a bit longer. We drove back to London. The flight home and a final year in engineering awaited. The connections to my summer adventure at Harwell, in Oxford, and to Maggie, were pulling free.

Two days later, I boarded the plane for my flight home. I caught a glimpse of Windsor Castle as we climbed away from Heathrow, and images of the countryside in Oxfordshire and Gloucestershire spooled in my mind as we headed west over England. It was a clear day. Ireland drifted past beneath us and then we began the long grind across the Atlantic.

It seemed natural to try to summarize the more than four months I had spent in Europe. Images from my whirlwind passage through continental Europe scrolled from memory. The eight weeks I had spent in England left a lasting impression, and elements of that time returned strongly, driven by the realization that I was now leaving it all behind. I had spent a most memorable time in Oxford, I had learned something about English life, I had met quite a few interesting people, and I was aware that all this had to be digested over the coming weeks. But I also had the sense that it was a time that had come and gone, and although it had been thoroughly enjoyable and I regretted it being over, it was over.

In fact, it was far from over. It would turn out to be barely the beginning of the beginning.

CHAPTER 3

TURNING POINT

Back in Toronto, I reconnected with those of my classmates who had advanced from third year to fourth year in chemical engineering. Since the summer hadn't produced the usual recharge of lucre in my bank account, I had to arrange a student loan for my final year's studies. But before that…

There were some bread-and-butter letters to write, thanking various people in England for their hospitality and their help in making my summer there a success. There was my cousin in Harrow, my supervisor and colleagues at Harwell, my landlady in Walton Crescent in Oxford, my friend Robert, and (after some reflection) Maggie's parents in Stroud to thank them for showing a complete stranger a lovely day.

I also wrote to Maggie to say how much I had enjoyed her company and to see whether she was interested in corresponding over the coming months. Maggie had been generous with her time, had delivered hours of lively conversation, had engaged in a good deal of the intelligent wordplay and sophisticated nonsense that I found so intriguing in England, and had made me familiar with quite a few aspects of Oxford. I expected that she would say yes to a brief correspondence, but that it would fade away naturally after a few exchanges of letters. I knew that she had her own career interests, and I had to decide what my life would look like after I graduated. I was intrigued by the possibility of finding a job on either coast in Canada. But I was aware that going from university to a working life would be a big change that would need some serious thought and planning.

Maggie and I did correspond, an exchange of letters about every six weeks or so. I settled into my final year in engineering. My impression from Maggie's letters was that she was enjoying her third and final year at Exeter. I began looking at possibilities following my graduation. By November, I had diagnosed one of the sources of uneasiness or impatience that I had been feeling since my return from England. It was a kind of withdrawal symptom. In general, I had seen in England a way of life that, in some important ways, was notably different from what I had known up to then. Life in England, as I saw it, seemed to have a richer texture. And the way life was lived there seemed different as well. What caught my attention was the wide range of things people were interested in, the things they talked about, and how they talked about them, indicating to me that life in England somehow involved greater perception and had more depth. A good deal of this was given extra meaning and greater focus through the time I had spent with Maggie.

There were some important specifics. Bear in mind that as I write this, I'm reflecting on a time that is now more than fifty years in the past. In Toronto, back then, there was nothing like the general attitude that is present today (2022) for conserving and putting to use buildings and structures that have historical and cultural significance nor the desire for celebrating our past. In fact, back then, there was a mood among many politicians in Toronto just to bulldoze anything that was "old" and replace it by some modern cathedral to the church of the architecturally obscene. The contrast between what I saw around me in Toronto and what I had seen in England was stark, even after accounting for the novelty factor and the differences in depth of historical veneer.

Perhaps more immediate for me and what is often an item of high visibility for students, were the differences in drinking establishments in Toronto and Oxford and the pronounced differences in their associated social contexts. I had found that many of the pubs I visited were, for many people, primarily places that involved an active social life. The beer was good, and it was easy to strike up interesting conversations. In contrast, drinking establishments in early 1970s Toronto were usually little better than unimaginative watering holes serving pallid liquid that ought to have been put back into the horse. Turning up at one of those watering holes and expecting some interesting and intelligent conversation would be close to a guaranteed disappointment.

These were engaging reflections, but they were things that I had consigned to that catch-all box called "experience". Spending time in Europe, and especially in England, was something I was glad I had done, but I had come to the reluctant conclusion that it had been just a detour, not a main road to anywhere I might expect to aim at.

My year of study progressed. Correspondence with Maggie continued and I was a bit surprised that it hadn't shown signs of fading away. My fourth-year project took a lot of work, and it surprised me somewhat one morning to find that February was almost at an end. Sometime soon and certainly within the next three months, I would need to have some kind of plan going forward, a plan that would shift me from an academic context to a working-world context. Desultory searches offered uninspiring occupational futures, like pulp-and-paper mills in northern Ontario towns, chemical plants in Southwestern Ontario, a job in the on-again, off-again oil-and-gas industry in Alberta, or work at one of the provincial electrical utilities. Attractive opportunities near the Atlantic or Pacific were minimal. In due course, I just put the whole matter aside, determined to focus on final exams; what came next would be tomorrow's problem.

The grind of studying for final exams had begun. I felt that I had entered that dream world that seems always to sit astride the approach to a major life change. Having rejected any consideration of further work in graduate school, I was on the exit ramp from academia. And on the on ramp to...?

I had worked steadily during the year, but there were still long nights studying, floating through that misty realm that seems to enclose university year-end. I was feeling comfortable at my mastery of the course work and wasn't worried about the exams. But the "what comes next" conundrum continued to intrude into my thoughts.

I don't remember quite when it happened, but it was during one of those long study nights. My mind was a maelstrom of mass transfer coefficients, phase diagrams, unit operations, Gibbs free energies — and so clogged with all that sort of exotica, in fact, that I'm surprised I heard the voice at all.

At first, it was just a sense of having missed something. I was certain there was no aspect of my course materials that I had neglected seriously, so I dismissed this as just a vague concern having no basis. But the feeling that something was missing persisted, and in fact became stronger. I deliberately put studying aside in order to face down this question, whatever it was. That's when the voice spoke to me.

"You don't want to let this one get away, Weaver."

It took little time to realize that "this one" was Maggie and that images of the time I had spent with Maggie were not going to disappear from my thoughts. And I had to figure out how to respond to that.

When I had spent a few days reflecting on all this, a course of action presented itself to me in a way that was seemingly spontaneous. I decided to write to Maggie once more. And I wrote out a letter right then. After which I returned to my studying with a clear mind.

The exams went about as I expected. In due course, I received official-looking correspondence telling me I now had the right to place a few letters after my name. The day of graduation was fixed, as was the date of another ceremony, unique to Canadian engineering schools, known as "The Ritual of the Calling of an Engineer". My relatives turned up at Convocation Hall the day of my graduation ceremony, pictures were taken of me in my gown and funny hat on the lawn of King's College Circle. My mother beamed proudly, my Aunt Alma was in tears, and then I took them to lunch and we talked about what I planned to do, something I had shared with my mother a few weeks earlier.

"So. I guess you leave soon, don't you?" my mother said, perhaps hoping there had been a change in plan, but as usual not raising any barriers. My mother knew what I had planned in general. I hadn't told her about the letter I had written to Maggie during that late night of studying, the letter that suggested a return to England.

"Yes. In three days time", I said. I didn't say anything about my role of best man at a good friend's wedding during those three days. Even as I related my three-day deadline, I realized that I had to consider my mother and my aunt much more seriously. Once I thought about it, I realized that to them, my graduation and impending departure into the world meant more than just some formulaic notion of "young fleeing the nest". I realized that at some level they must be feeling that something was being lost. I immediately insisted that I take them both out for a slap-up dinner. We did that, and there was a good bit of heart-to-heart talking.

My mother and my aunt both asked me about my upcoming trip. It seemed straightforward, but the air was full of unasked questions.

"It's something I have to do", I said finally, hoping that their intuition would save me having to stumble around, trying to explain something of which I myself really had no clear understanding. They both nodded and smiled more.

It had taken little time to make the arrangements. Maggie had reacted to my letter with interest. I had done the necessary background work. There would be no impediments or nasty barriers at Customs or Immigration in London, as far as I could see. As a completely unexpected surprise, an uncle had jumped the gun a couple of months before my final exams and had given me a generous financial "reward" for being the first person in our extended family to graduate from university. I had a long chat with him and thanked him for his confidence. That financial injection made it possible even to think of another trip to Europe.

"You'll be flying to London?" my mother asked.

"Yes."

"How long will you stay there?"

"I don't know. But once I find out you'll be the first to know."

That memorable day ended, I sold some of my textbooks and put a few others and my notes into storage, collected my airline ticket, donated some of my clothes to charity, and moved out of my student accommodation.

My mother came to the airport. She was still brimming with pride over her son, "the graduate", and although she was reluctant to see me leave, she exerted no pressure, raised no roadblocks to my plans, displayed the same parental support to my present decision as she had to all previous major decisions. She had known about Maggie since my return from England the previous autumn, and it some-times seemed that she could sense, in clearer terms than I did, that something important had happened for me. We talked about what I was doing, that maybe things wouldn't work out, but that I was going to see whether this was where my future lay.

I didn't refer to a turning point.

But I knew that just such a point was on the horizon. What I didn't know was which way I would be turning once I reached the point.

When one decides to strike out on a new adventure, a powerful tingle of excitement can take over. Metaphorical uplands bathed in sunlight, vistas previously unknown and now offering invitation and challenge can present themselves. Everything is essence of opportunity and enticement. The lure of a bright future prevents any possible downside from taking centre stage. Barriers are there to be broken, crashed through in pursuit of one's obvious destiny. It's all there for the taking, and nothing more than guts and optimism is required.

But then, paradoxically, when all preparations are completed, when one is armed for battle and hyped to win and feeling secure that one's own resources are more than sufficient, at just that point when one should be savouring forthcoming victory, doubts can seep in. I was in a state of high expectation as I boarded the plane. We taxied to the runway, the engines roared, we accelerated and then rose into the sky. A great adventure beckoned and I was on my way.

My particular Shakespearean "rub" soon kicked in. Transatlantic flights take a long time but adrenalin highs are transient. Night soon engulfed the plane. Moonlight reflected off the wing outside my window. The life I had known up to then was sliding into the darkness behind us. I was hurtling through empty, cold, featureless, moonlit space toward ... what?

I was surprised, shocked, and chastened to find strange and unwelcome thoughts filling my head. I was on a one-way trip, leaving behind everything I knew. The future before me was not just uncertain, it was unknown. A deep and implacable hesitation was overwhelming my being. Visions of old men dying alone in foreign countries began to haunt me. The only thing that stopped me thinking, *Is this a good idea?* was the fact that even if it wasn't a good idea, it was too late now to do anything about it. Lights in the cabin were dimmed. All around me, people were falling asleep. They all seemed so unconcerned, so relaxed. What did they know that I didn't? Surreal images floated...

This was back when British Airways was known as BOAC, back in the days of the allure of international flights, of youthful but worldly flight attendants and of their undoubtedly exciting lives, of a "jet set" existence. For some reason, I felt myself suddenly being dragged into that world unprepared. The voice of a young English woman reached me through my stupor.

"Some breakfast, sir?"

I blinked uncomprehendingly, feeling like a downed boxer at the referee's count of six. I looked around, tried to rise from the mat. The cabin lights were on. Glancing out the window, I could see an expanse of green below. Right! I was on an airplane. And I realized where I was going. Was that Ireland below? Good God, we'd soon be there! The fears and hesitation of a few hours ago were forgotten. I said yes to breakfast.

We cruised above the Bristol Channel, over Southern England, all the while dropping slowly toward Heathrow. As we descended, I noticed something that I would see many times subsequently, the streamers of condensed vapour that hugged the airflow over the wing. Then there was the whole rigmarole of landing, taxiing for what seemed miles, leaving the airplane, going through customs, collecting bags, and locating the bus to Central London. From the previous year, I remembered the feeling of gritty eyes and sleep-fogged brain but was focussed just on reaching the air terminal. We would wait to see what came after that.

The bus left Heathrow and jogged and wound its way into Central London. It was a gorgeous day, fluffy clouds making the blue sky seem even more radiant. I took in the buildings that passed by the bus window, sights that were familiar if not exactly recognizable from the previous summer. I must have been daydreaming because the bus pulled to a stop before I expected, and the driver announced, "Victoria Air Terminal, all change." I had contact information for Maggie at Exeter, and I had a vague plan to find somewhere to stay in London for a day, contact Maggie, and then figure out what to do in the short term. My "objective" in coming back to London was "not to let this one get away", but now that I was in London it was clear that I really had nothing at all worthy of being called a "plan". It was just some vague romantic notion. Worse, it was less than vague, the best description of it being "groundless". But now that I was here I would have to make the best of things and hope not to look like a complete moron.

I was travelling fairly light, so I retrieved my one smallish case from the bus and looked around, apparently expecting an answer to be written somewhere on a wall.

Buy a newspaper, I thought, failing to come up with anything more original. And I headed for a newsagent off to the right.

Glancing around, I noticed a brown miniskirt, a pale-tan blouse, a familiar haircut, and a brilliant smile.

"Hello, sailor", Maggie said.

"Hi, Maggie. I didn't expect to see you here. I was going to—"

She reached up and hugged me, and we swayed there for a few seconds.

"I wasn't sure what you might have in mind", she said through a friendly smile, "so I brought a toothbrush and a spare pair of knickers."

By this time, it was well after eleven o'clock.

"How about some lunch?" I offered rather lamely.

"Okay. Where?"

"There's a good place just down Buckingham Palace Road. A restaurant called Bumbles."

"Wow! Fresh off the boat but already he has all the moves!" Her eyes twinkled impishly.

We had a long lunch in Bumbles and brought each other up to date while I tried for conversation that would avoid a demonstration that I had no real plan whatever. I mumbled something about finding a bedsit and taking next steps. Maggie listened to my mumbling, then offered her own suggestion.

"Why don't you come back with me to Exeter. Right now. My graduation is coming up, and I need to get ready to move out of our flat."

It dawned on me then that, although Maggie's parents were not impoverished, she was a student nonetheless and unlikely to have received a windfall from a doting uncle. So I would have to shoulder the financial burden.

The Exeter plan was appealing. I paid for our lunch over some objections, and we headed off to Paddington Station. At the ticket wicket, I bought our tickets to Exeter, again over some objections. Soon we were on the train.

When I asked Maggie about her final year at university ("uni"), about how it went, her face clouded over somewhat.

"I know I didn't do as well as I wanted to. Probably will be a disappointment to my mother."

I remembered Maggie's mother, Joan, from the previous summer. A woman to be reckoned with. Well informed, well read, intelligent, but all of it worn lightly. I had the sense, from our short one-day acquaintance, that she and I shared some connection. Or was that just a sense of intrigue at something different?

We talked about my year.

"Nothing much to say", I replied. "Lots of boring technical stuff. Got a good degree. But now that I'm finished with academia, I'm not sure just what 'good' means."

Maggie looked out the window. The train was now cruising through London's outer fringes.

"And now you're back here", Maggie said, turning to face me again.

It was phrased as a statement, but was really an open-ended question, one that I wasn't sure how to answer. The drinks-and-sandwiches trolley came past, and I took that as an opportunity to stall. I asked if Maggie wanted anything but she shook her head. I ordered a soft drink, fumbled with some coins, opened the can, and took a sip. I delayed further, looked down at my hands, then gazed out the train window. Windsor Castle drifted by in the distance.

"You might remember", I began, "that I said in one of my letters that my time in England and Europe last summer was an eye-opener for me. I had never encountered so much that was new and different and significant before."

Maggie waited for me to continue.

"So I felt I needed to come back here to see what it was that was so significant, take a closer look."

I was making a hash of all this, avoiding what it was that I really should be saying, afraid that in being too direct I might spook her. Somewhere there was a hope that I could dodge all that. If things turned out the way they ought to, spending time with Maggie in Exeter could indicate a way forward or show that there really was no way forward.

"I'll have a few days in Exeter before anything important needs to happen", Maggie said. "We can do a little local touring. If you'd be interested in that."

I agreed to this as a short-term plan that would rescue me from more fumbling, and we began chatting about less consequential matters.

The train was slowing now as we approached Reading. People began rising from their seats, dragging bags and briefcases from the overhead racks. The train stopped in the station, and through the open upper windows, a woman's voice made the arrival announcement over the station Tannoy in what seemed to me an absurdly strained plummy delivery. Maggie had the same sense, it appeared. A frown darkened her face.

"What's the matter with her?" Maggie asked of nobody in particular.

A man seated across from us smiled in agreement. Mentally, I found myself suddenly back in Oxford, recalling instances of Maggie's forthrightness and impatience at things she didn't understand and couldn't see a good reason for. And I recalled thinking, at the time back then in Oxford, how this definite and decisive approach to things was in such contrast to the hesitancy and vagueness that seemed more typical of members of my family, an apparent congenital unwillingness to take a firm stance in any situation, important or otherwise, where a decision was required. This had been something that left me impatient from the age of about sixteen onward, and I resolved early on that in my own behaviour I would break that mould. Was that part of what had appealed to me about Maggie in Oxford?

The train pulled out of Reading a few minutes later. Maggie and I talked about our university experiences in general, and I recalled how pleasant it had been meeting her parents that one day the previous September, and then we lapsed into companionable silence.

The train gave a sudden shudder and I snapped half awake.

"Another train", Maggie said, "going the other way." I looked at my watch. More than an hour had elapsed since I was last aware of the time.

"Sorry", I said. "I must have fallen asleep. Where are we?" Not that the answer would have meant much to me. But in my barely conscious state, it seemed a reasonable thing to ask.

"Not exactly sure where we are. Probably not far from Bristol. Won't be too much longer now. You're obviously jet-lagged, so nothing to apologize for. How do you feel?"

"Surprisingly good, in fact." And I roused myself a bit, sat up in the seat, rubbed a now whiskery face, and resolved to try to stay awake for the rest of the trip. And in that I was successful.

"Tell me a bit about Exeter."

"It has a nice small university. That's why I chose it. Far enough away from home but not too far. Nice countryside. Lots of history. We'll explore some of it."

The train was passing through delightful countryside, and I just sat and watched it flow past, almost mesmerized. Maggie and I drifted in and out of conversation as the train continued galloping toward Exeter. On trains in Europe I have always tended to lose track of time, so I was not expecting it when Maggie rose from her seat.

"We'll be coming into the station at Exeter in a few minutes", she said, and this was confirmed by the conductor's announcement almost immediately after.

I was curious about the station name, St. David's, but decided to pursue that later. The train stopped, and we made our way onto the platform and out of the station.

"It's not far to my flat. We can walk. My two flatmates have left already. I said I'd deal with the landlord for them."

"There must be a pub or B&B where I can get a room", I said.

Maggie gave me a funny look.

"What's wrong with my flat?"

I decided there was absolutely nothing wrong with Maggie's flat.

"We can drop our things there. We need something for our local tour. And we need to get something for dinner tonight."

I had thought of suggesting a restaurant, but that and other options clearly had been bypassed. The flat was a fairly typical student accommodation, but clean, light, airy, and pleasant. We went out again almost immediately, did some shopping, and Maggie bought a large sheet of plastic. Expecting that all would become obvious soon enough, I asked no questions. We took everything back to the flat, then set out for a short walk around Exeter. It was an attractive city, somewhat impoverished in places, but Maggie seemed to know it well and kept up a commentary on what we were seeing. We walked for about an hour, but when I failed to suppress a yawn, Maggie responded immediately.

"Oh, sorry. You must be knackered. We should get back and have an early dinner."

And so we went back to Maggie's flat, I demonstrated at least modest familiarity with a kitchen as we prepared together what Maggie referred to as a "rice mush", then we sat down to it along with a bottle of white wine that I had insisted on buying when we were shopping. We clinked chunky wine tumblers, I smiled across at Maggie over wine and food, and it was clear to me that Maggie was entirely relaxed about our situation. We finished the wine, cleared away the dishes, and washed up. As I dried the last plate, I tried but failed to suppress another yawn.

Maggie smiled, took the tea towel from me, and undid the top buttons of my shirt.

"Time for bed", she said.

There followed a wonderful and extended repeat of the one time we had made love in Oxford.

It seemed indeed that a turning point had been reached, and that the possibility of a path forward was now much more likely.

CHAPTER 4

PIGEONS, PIGLETS, PONDERING

As I write this in May of 2022, a piece of music surges powerfully in my memory. It's a two-minute, forty-eight-second recording of an organ work composed by Eugène Gigout, his Toccata in B Minor. It's lovely and lively, but it speaks to me also, and maybe principally, because the CD version of it that I have was recorded in Buckfast Abbey. How Buckfast Abbey enters this story will become clear.

Maggie and I rose early the next morning and had a breakfast of bacon and eggs, something I soon learned was one of Maggie's perennial favourite meals. Then we loaded a small backpack with changes of underwear, socks, shirts, toilette items, several boiled eggs, and buttered bread rolls. We packed two sleeping bags so that they were easily transportable as one bundle and left the flat. A local train took us south to Dawlish, and Maggie showed me around an area that is not only a local tourist haunt but was also a common weekend tryst for Exeter students. Maggie seemed to have a sheaf of timetables for local buses, and we roamed in lovely vehicles in a leisurely way through that part of Devon south and west of Exeter. The lanes were narrow, winding, and very attractive, and they led through impossibly bucolic villages. I felt the urge to stop at every pub, most of them being gorgeous, but settled for patronizing just a few. Maggie was quite taken by how I was drawn to these country alehouses, but she was familiar with them whereas I had spent no time in rural Devon.

At every one of our pub stops, we sat outdoors in settings that were quiet and peaceful on account of there being so little traffic. Calmly sipping a pint of local beer or cider, sharing a serving of chips with Maggie, and listening to birds in the trees all around us, I felt transported. Being a Gloucestershire lass, Maggie was at home in all this, although I was reminded at regular intervals that she was far from being just a demure country maid. At one pub, as I sat sipping and ruminating, there was the sound of a lot of energetic flapping coming from somewhere, but looking around, I couldn't see what was causing it.

"What's that?" I inquired idly.

Maggie's reply was straightforward and factual, not intending to be anything other than that: "Pigeons copulating."

At one point we decided to walk from a village where a local bus dropped us to another village two or three miles away, where we could board another local bus. We followed a few lanes, then diverted across a field when we noticed signs for a footpath. The path led from some downland into a shallow valley, and we passed a gate across a farmer's access route into one of his fields. We gazed over the gate into the field, and suddenly a group of small animals was rushing toward us.

"Piglets!" Maggie exclaimed, completely charmed. The piglets, at least a dozen of them, and probably not more than a few weeks old, ran up to the gate, which they couldn't pass, then milled around squealing and snorting, apparently looking for us to give them something to eat. We reached in and touched them, and they squealed some more. I recall clearly the look on Maggie's face, one of sheer childlike delight.

The next bus we caught took us to the town of Buckfastleigh, and from there we walked the short distance to Buckfast Abbey. Originally Benedictine, it became Cistercian in the twelfth century. Buckfast Abbey suffered like all other abbeys in England during the reign of

Henry VIII and his dissolution of the monasteries. But Buckfast Abbey was rebuilt in the nineteenth century. Maggie and I spent some time looking at the abbey and its grounds, and then we found a spot in the grass where we could sit and eat our boiled eggs and bread rolls. We could hear someone playing the organ inside. The place left me stunned. Here was a beautiful structure deep in the English country-side, an indication of what had been evidently an important local centre in a way of life from centuries ago, but almost all that way of life was now long gone. And yet the abbey itself remained a cul-tural reality present here and now. I hesitated to say anything, being aware that comments on aspects of European culture coming from North Americans can sound gauche and immature. I didn't want to risk branding myself that way. Maggie obviously noticed that I was examining everything around me closely.

"Makes you think, doesn't it?" she said.

Over the more than half century I knew Maggie, it was always clear to me that she tried to be aware of what others felt and to be sympathetic to those feelings. Her response that day outside Buckfast Abbey was just one facet of that awareness.

We roamed further on local buses, into the late afternoon, when we headed for a spot on the coast not far from Paignton. We found a suitable place to spend the night, on a grassy incline just above a small stretch of shingle beach and less than a mile from a nice-looking small pub where we could get dinner. At the pub, we were met by smiles and presumed to be students doing some local exploring, likely on a financial shoestring, and carrying a backpack and a rolled sleeping bag. Maggie discovered that the pub menu offered gammon steak and broad beans, another of her favourite meals. So we had two orders of gammon steaks and two pints of very good cider. I watched Maggie out of the corner of my eye as she ate. It was an image of complete youthful enjoyment.

Back at our campsite, we zipped the sleeping bags together, and I discovered why Maggie had bought the large sheet of plastic. At some point, she had stitched it together to form a giant sausage that fit around the outside of the sleeping bags.

"Might rain", she said. "Might be heavy dew. Might be gull droppings."

I pulled out two packets of Twiglets that I had bought when I had paid for our dinner at the pub. We sat on the sleeping bag, munched

Twiglets, listened to waves chattering on the shingle beach, and enjoyed a warm sunset.

Fresh air, cider, a good meal, and some walking did the trick and appeared to be the only creature comforts we needed. As we climbed into the sleeping bag, I was very aware of Maggie's body, but we were both asleep pretty much as soon as we put our heads down. The night seemed to pass in an instant. I awoke first. The air was cold, the sky swirled pink and purple, and the sea was quiet.

But I became alarmed almost instantly. The tide was coming in! The water was lapping just a few inches from our feet. The sleeping bag wasn't wet, but it might be only a matter of minutes.

I woke Maggie and outlined the problem. She looked around.

"No. The tide's not the problem. See, there's more shingle now than there was last night. The plastic sheet has just slid down across the grass. But another hour and we might have launched."

Her eyes twinkled. She looked around. "I think we have time", she said. Half an hour later, we climbed out of the sleeping bag and got dressed.

We spent the next two days working our way back to Exeter, once again mostly on rural buses. The first day took us to Torquay, and we spent a few hours walking along the waterfront and in the town's central area. A pub ploughman's lunch was taken inside because of on-again, off-again showers. On another local bus, we followed a delightful roundabout route to Teignmouth where we found a tucked-away pub that had a room for the night, an option made appealing because of the threat of some serious overnight rain. We dodged showers during the afternoon in Teignmouth, spent an hour in a used bookshop, then decided to flop and read our books in our room to avoid the rain. The pub had a good kitchen and our evening meals of fish and chips were excellent. I bought two cans of Blackthorn Cider, which we sipped in our room.

I knew that Maggie's exam results would be posted sometime the next day, so we would be going back to Exeter by local bus to Dawlish, then the rest of the way by train. I couldn't really tell what Maggie was thinking about her exam results; they would indicate what level of degree she would receive. Then there would be the graduation ceremony, and Maggie's parents would come down from Stroud for that. When they saw that I was in Exeter, they would likely draw the obvious conclusion, and I had to decide what I would say. I hoped it would be clear enough to anyone looking in from the outside that here were two young people assessing options. In response to any questions, I would need to come out with something vague but not too vague. But the situation was fluid, and beyond Maggie's graduation, any details going forward were foggy.

Lying side by side on the bed reading, Maggie lowered her book and looked at me.

"What comes next?" she asked simply.

I knew what that meant.

"I plan to go to London, find a place to stay, and find something to do."

"Why London?"

"It seems the best place to start", I said. "Much better chance of finding something there, I expect."

"I might not end up in London", Maggie said. "Plenty of places besides London where I could look for a job."

I shrugged. "Well, I'm prepared to take it one step at a time. If you are as well."

"What about us?" Maggie asked bluntly.

"I'm prepared to take that one step at a time too. And I want to keep taking those steps."

Maggie looked at me for a longish time, smiled faintly, said, "Okay", and went back to reading her book.

At eight thirty, it was clear that a full day, a good dinner, and two cans of nice cider meant that we were ready to go to sleep.

The next morning we awoke almost simultaneously, looked at each other, and decided without having to say anything that lust could be put on hold for the time being. The pub did a decent breakfast, but we settled for just toast and a few slices of lovely Devon bacon. By nine o'clock, we were back outside waiting for our next country bus.

And on that bus, we rambled through some picture-postcard countryside, stopped at a pub next to a cricket green where we enjoyed a Scotch egg and a pint each, hopped on the next bus, and arrived midafternoon at Dawlish. The local train deposited us in Exeter just before four o'clock.

I could tell that Maggie was feeling nervous. She had become increasingly quiet during the afternoon, and I guessed that she was concerned over what her exam results would reveal. But she led the way to where the results would be posted, displaying what one might call brave resolve. I stood back as she scanned down the sheets listing names and results.

"Oh bugger!" Maggie exclaimed. "They've given me a pass degree!"

I put my hand on her shoulder but she sloughed it off. She wasn't in tears, but she was close to it.

We stood there for a moment while Maggie gazed at nothing in particular. Without turning to look at me, she then said, "Buy me a drink!"

I guessed that the nearest half-decent pub would do. We found one, entered, and Maggie took a seat while I went to the bar. They had a respectable white wine open, so I ordered two glasses and took them back to our table. Maggie sipped and cast an unfocussed gaze across the pub. I guessed that she was navigating a private space.

"My mother won't be impressed."

It was a statement of personal disappointment and reflected how much her parents' esteem, and particularly her mother's, meant to her. They would be here in Exeter for the graduation ceremony, to see her presented the lowest-grade university degree available, having watched others collect their firsts and upper seconds. It was a little chastening for me to recognize that there was nothing I could do to share this moment or cushion its impact. I was just a friend, and a friend of not very well-defined status.

We finished our wine, and Maggie said, "I'm going back to the flat." We made our way there wordlessly. As we approached the door, Maggie turned to me and said, "I'd like to be on my own for a while."

I nodded. "Okay. I'll be back in a few hours."

Maggie unlocked the door. "Here. Take my key", she said, handing it to me.

I wanted to give Maggie a hug, but the look on her face said no.

So I walked. A harsh voice inside said it was time to rethink this whole lark. Just what was I trying to do?

The answer seemed straightforward enough to me: something that seemed to offer a worthwhile life situation and needed to be explored. And I had come here to explore it. But I was outside the boundaries of my known physical and cultural world, trying to determine — what? Something. The exact nature of that something was vague. In general,

I had an idea what it was about, and in hand-waving terms, it would involve finding out whether Maggie and I were suited to be a couple. There were unknowns here. Had the eight weeks with Maggie in the previous year just been some kind of summer fling that would have no meaning if it were pasted onto a larger canvas? Maggie's family background and mine were quite different. We came from different cultural contexts, and I couldn't tell how much that difference might matter. I pondered all these things as I walked. Maybe we would find, after a few weeks, that it was all just a pipe dream, and the best thing would be simply for me to go back to Canada. Maybe we would find that we had quite a bit of the right stuff in common and that it would make sense to see where a relationship could lead. If so, maybe we would find that it was golden, magical, and that we were somehow meant to be. Maybe we would find that it all looked good but then soured quickly and would fall apart.

I walked on and thought of all this. Of course I wanted to believe that Maggie and I could fashion a good future. There was no way to work through this on the basis of logic. We would just need to try.

I had had no idea where I thought my cogitations might lead and felt that I had been pondering for not much more than half an hour. So I was surprised to see, when I checked my watch, that I had been walking for more than three hours. Likely it would take me more than half an hour to make my way back to Maggie's flat. Would she have begun to worry?

At a brisk walking pace, I made it back to Maggie's flat in forty minutes. I let myself in and started upstairs. I could hear Maggie's hurried steps coming down.

"There you are!" she said, taking my hand. "I was beginning to think you had an accident!" It looked as though she had been crying, although not recently, and I hoped not because I had caused her to worry or panic.

We went to Maggie's kitchen, exchanged a long hug, and I said yes to the offer of a cup of coffee. Sitting at the kitchen table, hands gripping my coffee mug, I told Maggie what I had been pondering during my walk. She listened without interrupting.

"Sounds awfully serious", she said.

"Well, I suppose it is, if I take a long view. But if it all works out the way I hope, it's likely to be quite a trip."

Maggie was still feeling sombre about her pass degree, evidently. She turned her coffee cup round one way and then back. I noticed her hands. Small. Delicate. Almost like a child's hands. The thought occurred that she was "only" twenty-one years old. She had had perhaps six years to form thoughts of life in an adult world, and I wondered how ready any of us are at that age to make the major decisions that go with all that. It was clear to me that in facing any such decision I had few relevant resources to fall back on.

"You mean making all the right decisions, being happy, having a life?" Maggie's expression as she said this was somewhere between sceptical and mocking.

"Yes. But there's no grand plan. It's not a fine calculation that's either right or wrong. It's a question of try it and see."

Maggie looked at me steadily, then a slow smile crept across her face, a smile I would get to know very well.

"Sounds like you've swotted up on this."

I had to smile in my turn.

"Yes. I'm being too earnest, aren't I?" I said.

"Well", Maggie began, "only by half", she said once again through her sly smile.

I took a long sip of my coffee and put the mug down carefully.

"I guess the answer has to be a curry. I'll get them and be right back." And I began to rise.

"What?" Maggie said, suddenly looking puzzled. "Curry?"

I stood, shifting impatiently, glanced at my watch, looked at her steadily but expressionlessly.

"Ah! You're hungry", she concluded. "Well, I guess I am too. Let's not do takeout. I'll come down too." Maggie rose from her chair. The sly smile was back. "I guess you're feeling pretty crafty."

"Who? Me?"

Maggie waved that one off in mock impatience. She pulled on her shoes and we went out into the evening and had a nice curry and a pint of lager each. We then returned to Maggie's flat and settled in the sitting room to read our books.

I must have become engrossed in what I was reading. Suddenly, I realized that Maggie was standing over me.

"I'm tired", she said.

It turned out that she wasn't tired. But she needed something to compensate for the downer of her pass degree. A large measure of TLC was in order.

The day of Maggie's graduation finally arrived. Her parents were there. I was there and was a bit surprised that Maggie's parents did no double takes and asked no questions when I met them again and we shook hands.

The ceremony went off without a hitch. Maggie got her piece of paper. And that was pretty much it. Maggie's parents went home again. I stayed in Exeter another day and helped Maggie pack her remaining clothes into a suitcase. We went out for one more dinner, had one more night in her flat, and then we went our ways, she to Stroud where she would stay briefly, and me to London where I would try to figure out what came next.

CHAPTER 5

FINDING COMMON GROUND

My trip to London was strange. Nothing to do with the trip itself, just to do with me — meaning that I hadn't yet become used to the idea of what it was I was trying to do. I tried to convince myself that things were better than I felt them to be, that I had just fallen under a shadow. But the shadow stayed where it was.

The immediate tasks were obvious and had to be done in any case. I would find a place to stay, try to find some sort of work, and then talk to Maggie, see where to go from there. If anywhere.

It was good to arrive at Paddington Station not at rush hour, and by the time I stepped off the train, I had a plan. Sort of. I bought a *London A to Z* and a newspaper at the WH Smith newsstand, found a bench in an out-of-the-way corner of the station, and began looking at ads for rooms to rent. I wanted something close to good railway or tube connections and I found four possibilities. A visit to a nearby bank provided me a supply of coins. I found a telephone box and began calling. None of the four was available any longer, which gave me the hint that successful bedsit hunters were early birds, and anything decent would be gone by midmorning. I found a cheap hotel not far from the station and took a room by the day.

Bedsit hunting was a disheartening experience. For three days, I checked newspapers, thumbed through the *A to Z*, made telephone calls, and trekked to prospective bedsits. More than half of them I turned down just on first sight, and during what was left of each of those three days, I did some desultory wandering, found quite a few interesting pubs, and read cheap novels in my rent-by-the-day room.

The fourth day yielded a harvest of six places to visit, three of them I rejected out of hand, two turned out to be too far from good public transport, and I headed off to the sixth place under lowering skies and through a discouraging drizzle. The house was in Wandsworth, an area of London about which I knew nothing, and was part of a row of terrace houses in a small street named Jessica Road. Number 14. I was approaching drowned-rat status when I arrived there, but I shook the excess water from my hair, brushed it off my leather jacket, and rang the doorbell. A pleasant woman of Indian descent opened the door. I introduced myself and she invited me in.

The place was lovely, well-kept, clean, utilitarian, and was just what I wanted, so I expressed a desire to take it straight away.

"Well, I can't offer it to you immediately. There's another prospective tenant, Dr. Dile, who'll be getting back to me this afternoon. If he turns it down, I'd be happy for you to move in."

I took an immediate dislike to this Dr. Dile.

She gave me a number I could call after 3:00 p.m. I thanked her and set out again in the rain, not looking forward to more of the same the next day.

I phoned her at 3:05 p.m. Dr. Dile had declined, thereby becoming quite a nice guy. I asked if I could move in that afternoon. She said I could, so I collected my things from my grotty little hotel room, informed the tired man on the ground floor that I wouldn't be staying that night, and was off to Wandsworth again.

It was a surprise how much relief I felt at having a room of "my own". This was 1971, the rent was £7 a week, something not even imaginable today. Although very little had changed over the course of a few hours, my mood had gone from down in the dumps to almost euphoric. I turned up again in Jessica Road, paid a week's rent, got my key, unpacked, and made myself at home. During these exchanges, I learned that Dr. Dile didn't really exist. He was a name invoked by my landlady as a holding action whenever she was considering tenants, something to give her a few hours to consider in private. But I decided that Dr. Dile probably was still okay.

"Home" consisted of one large room containing a bed, a small dresser, two chairs, and a table that could be used either for eating or working. The room was on the third floor; next door to it was a communal kitchen available for use by me and the other tenant, whose room was one landing down. On the next landing below that, there were the communal toilet and bathroom.

Although it was getting ahead of things somewhat, I wondered whether this was the sort of place that Maggie might feel at home in. It wasn't all that different from the room she had in the flat in Exeter: three rooms for the three young women who shared, and a communal kitchen and bathroom. On that basis I concluded that likely it would do.

I sat down immediately to write a letter to Maggie giving her my new address. That letter would be mailed first thing in the morning when I would set out to look for a job. I had nothing I could use to prepare a meal, and it was too late to go shopping now, so I just headed out to find a decent local pub. That turned out to be not a problem. A small pub in St. John's Hill leading toward Clapham Junction looked attractive. The chalkboard on the bar showed three menu items, and I was pleased to see that toad-in-the-hole was one of them. This was a dish that Maggie had introduced me to. A quiet murmur filled the pub. A half-dozen men of varying ages supported the bar, gazing into their pints as though seeking inspiration on some obscure mathematical theorem. An older lady sat by herself nursing a half pint of Guinness. The publican looked about sixty, had an engaging smile, and displayed a kind of scrubbed-pink cherubic look. Recognizing immediately that I wasn't English, he asked me where I came from and what I was doing, and we had a pleasant chat while I waited for my toad. This little pub, The Beehive, would become Maggie's and my local in Wandsworth.

For the remainder of that evening, I lay on my bed, enjoyed a novel by Alistair Maclean, and smiled at my new home.

Over the next few days the pace changed. I got a letter from Maggie saying that she had landed a job at a library association called Aslib, the Association of Special Libraries, and that she would be working in Belgrave Square. The Aslib job was the beginning of Maggie's working career. And it was work that Maggie loved. The pay was low, but that didn't matter to someone just starting out. Maggie's Aslib job was good news for me, since we would both be in London.

It took Maggie essentially no time at all to slip into her work, an indication perhaps that she was a natural in that field but also that her instincts were spot on. Within just a few weeks, she was entirely at home in Aslib. I remember being struck by this and, looking back, I had to wonder whether Maggie considered, even in those early days, that Aslib was a possibility for long-term employment. We never really discussed it. But I suspect that an early intention would have been to stay there many years. As soon became evident in her working life, Maggie had many talents, and her various interests came together in ways that yielded surprising results, and I believe that she began to outgrow Aslib as she gained experience, learned new aspects of information work, and as her understanding of the pervasive role of information in her world deepened. At that time, Maggie's work and life in London were not driven by high expectations. As I look back, I can see that we were enjoying the life of two young people in a great and exciting city.

My own search for work had struck low-grade ore. I had gone out looking for anything, and anything was just about what I had found. I discovered that there was all sorts of work for people who didn't mind what they had to do. So I got occasional work in a construction yard, for a small landscaping operation, as a driver's mate on a beer delivery truck, doing heavy or dirty work as it came along in several pubs, and shelf stocking in the local grocery store. None of these jobs paid a lot, and they turned up at unpredictable times for a few hours or a few days, but they brought in a little more money than I needed and avoided me having to plunder the store of my uncle's cash I had brought with me from Toronto.

Another letter from Maggie told me the day and time she would be arriving at Paddington Station — and could I meet her.

And I did. She stepped down from the carriage and came along the platform, wearing the big smile that I was getting to know well.

"Where to?" I asked.

"Let's go to your place. I have nowhere else to go."

I asked when she would start her new job, and she said on Monday, which was four days away.

"I'll need to find my own place", Maggie said, offering it as a simple statement of fact.

"You think you won't like my place? Or maybe Wandsworth is too much a down-at-heel address?" — me offering them as just questions of fact.

"No", Maggie said. "My mother will want to know that I'm established, which means knowing my address. It can't be your address."

I found no reply to that.

"A place of my own doesn't need to be much. Just call it a polite fiction."

We travelled across London, and Maggie was pleased at what was before her when we turned into Jessica Road. The street was little travelled by cars, it was close to Wandsworth Common, it was nicely treed, and it had a look of near-affluent lower middle class. Maggie and my landlady, Mrs. Brown, took to each other at once. Maggie talked briefly about Exeter and Aslib and explained that she would like to camp with me for a day or two until she found a place of her own. If that was okay. Mrs. Brown just smiled and said, "Of course", then invited us to have some tea with her. I hadn't been sure about all this, and to have this first step of our London adventure fall into place so easily was a pleasant experience.

Maggie did find her own place almost right away. It was a tiny bedsit in the home of a retired widow who was clearly in no financial distress and said to Maggie eventually that she just wanted to know there would be someone else in the house from time to time. It was indeed "from time to time" since Maggie spent many nights at my place. About six weeks later, Maggie was contacted by one of her school friends from Stroud. They had kept in contact, and Lisa was looking for two or more women who would share a place in London with her. It all just came together, and they found a flat in New Cross, close to Goldsmiths College where Lisa was studying. New Cross was a fair distance from Wandsworth, but it turned out that this posed no problem.

Maggie started work in Belgrave Square, fell into step with some sympathetic colleagues there, and found her Aslib feet quickly. It took little time for Maggie to begin developing expertise in her information work, and her ability at research, a great strength and a prominent advantage in all later jobs, shone through almost immediately. At Aslib, Maggie did work for members of the association, and these were scattered across London and throughout Britain. She took to the work right away and she loved it. The pay was low but the satisfaction level was high.

I continued doing whatever manual work I could find, but in parallel, I had begun looking for something more upscale. For ads on professional positions, I soon found that *The Daily Telegraph* was the paper to keep an eye on, and that the largest number of promising job advertisements seemed to appear on Wednesdays and Thursdays.

And so we settled into what turned out to be a temporary routine.

A good part of that routine involved exploration. There was Clapham Junction, a town centre as well as an interchange station through which commuter and main-line trains from both Victoria and Waterloo Stations passed. Clapham Junction once claimed the record for the largest number of parallel rails in one station.

At a point that was then still in the future, Maggie and I would board a train at Clapham Junction for Victoria Station every morning, but a clear memory of The Junction for me is an elegant old building that housed a department store known as Arding & Hobbs. That place had the most eclectic inventory of almost everything, and Maggie and I spent hours just poking around in it. We found saucepans, plates, a doorstop formed of cast iron in the shape of a snail, all kinds of storage jars (one of Maggie's particular weaknesses), silver toothpicks, shoe-horns of all lengths and designs, tea towels displaying railway memorabilia, wigs, frilly underwear for men, bin ends of stainless-steel cutlery that was elegant in its simplicity, garden implements, bird cages, cat toys, and just about anything else one could imagine. We equipped our kitchen and dining space from Arding & Hobbs. Our cutlery we kept jumbled in a drawer fitted into the small table in my room, a drawer that regularly stuck and would need to be coaxed into co-operating. Plates and mugs were stored on a makeshift shelf on the other side of the room. There were two small cupboards in the kitchen, one for me and one for Barry, the other tenant. How Maggie managed to produce her usual imaginative meals from such a humble working space I still can't imagine. But she did.

At Arding & Hobbs and elsewhere, Maggie showed the extent to which she always had other people in mind, by spotting something that X would like or that Y had been looking for. To Maggie, this kind of activity, noticing things that she could find a home for, was as natural as breathing.

The only physical remnants that I retain from that time are eight uncomplicated bread-and-butter knives we bought at Arding & Hobbs. They are now used to prepare meals for my cats.

Clapham Junction also had a Burton's Tailor, where some months later I shelled out £14 for a Harris Tweed jacket. The whole area is very much up-market now, but back then it hadn't yet shaken off its working-class background. The buildings looked tired and uncared for. The smoke from the many steam trains that had once passed through Clapham Junction had left stone and brickwork black and sooty. There were a few restaurants, but they were mostly greasy spoons, places where struggling pensioners would order cheap meals then quietly spoon most of what was on their plates into small plastic bags for careful consumption later, probably spread over a couple of days. I often think back to that time when Maggie and I were in jobs we enjoyed, when we had a small radio but no television, when entertainments were doing crossword puzzles and playing board games or other games that we invented. Very little was needed to be happy. But within the limits of our sparse accommodation, we were happy. I recall not caring all that much about whether jobs had a clear future direction. We hadn't yet developed any aspirations for a living arrangement more elaborate than what we had. I have clear recollections of the satisfaction derived from conversations in pubs when we sat and drank and joked and laughed with acquaintances of likewise nebulous status.

In total, together and individually, we spent almost four years in Jessica Road. During all that time, Maggie worked her magic on everything and everyone. Our landlady had become practically a confidante. The merchants where we did our shopping in the high street all waved, smiled, and greeted her. The couple who operated our local pub, The Beehive, beamed out a generous welcome whenever we entered.

We began to collect small stuffed toys made in the shape of animals to decorate small spaces in our flat. Maggie was intrigued by the stuffed toy known as an ookpik, and she actually found a small cloth ookpik somewhere. All our little animals had names, and the ookpik became known as Hippolyte. I don't remember why. We had a small carved marble bull named Ferdinand, an elegant slug in clear blue glass that Maggie named Sacha, a life-size stuffed puppy who was given the name Barclay, a hippopotamus called Jessica, a life-size toucan sporting the name Arthur, and two Dala horses we called Sven and Hendrik. Some of these "family members" we acquired while we were at Jessica Road; others came later.

There was one other "animal" that I wish now we had kept. He was named Mortimer, once again for reasons I have forgotten. In those days, Maggie wore pantyhose. It was a characteristic of those garments that ladders, known as "runs" in North America, would form in them, sometimes after having been worn only a couple of times. Ladders and the price of pantyhose both irritated Maggie, and in her typically pragmatic manner, she found a way around these twin problems. Whenever a ladder appeared in one leg of her pantyhose, Maggie would cut off that leg and keep both the amputated leg and the now one-legged hose. Eventually, there would be a ladder in the other leg of another set of pantyhose, and the same surgery would be applied. Maggie would now have two war-wounded pantyhose, one having only a left leg and the other having only a right leg. She would then pull on both allowing unladdered coverage of both her legs. Outwardly, it looked like she was wearing a single item of pantyhose. I asked her one time if that arrangement posed any problem.

"Makes me bum a bit warm. And it means that spending a penny involves a few more steps."

Eventually even each of the single-legged pantyhose would also develop a ladder. None of these killed-in-action undergarments nor the amputated legs was thrown out. They were used as stuffing. Maggie used pieces of old clothes to make a patchwork alligator (Mortimer) who was about three feet long. This alligator was stuffed using dead pantyhose pieces. It eventually took more than sixty sets of dead pantyhose parts to make this patchwork animal look like a well-fed pet. When I look back on it, Mortimer symbolizes for me the whimsical, thrifty, and inventive aspects of Maggie. In what is perhaps just some oddly distorted nostalgia, I really wish that I still had Mortimer.

Maggie soon became known to various people in Wandsworth. She developed an engaging banter with Vince, the local butcher. A tiny grocery store (it would be called a convenience store today), five minutes' walk from our place in Jessica Road, was operated by a man called Lee, and Maggie always congratulated him on offering competition to the monster supermarket Tesco just down the road, something that brought Lee out in giggles every time. Just across one corner of Wandsworth Common, in a small street named Elsynge Road, Maggie discovered that someone, Andy, who had attended Exeter with her, was sharing a flat with three other "blokes". Andy was a different sort of guy, very much a free spirit, someone who had no direction in life but was an amusing drinking partner. In those days, milk was still delivered daily to individual homes by means of small electric vans. The requested number of pint bottles of milk (having red, silver, or gold foil caps depending on butterfat content) would be left, and old empty bottles taken away, provided those empties had been washed. Andy and his flatmates had no interest in washing milk bottles, so they put them out dirty, and of course they weren't collected. The low brick walls leading from the street to the door of the house that contained their flat was lined, both sides, by at least fifty dirty milk bottles. It looked like a war of wills. Andy and his flatmates also had a small marijuana plant in a pot in their kitchen window. The plant died eventually because, as soon as the poor thing put out a new leaf, it was picked and smoked.

Visits by both of us to Elsynge Road were rare, since Maggie wasn't much impressed by the underwear, socks, and jeans that frequently littered the floor. The kitchen never really looked salubrious, and it wasn't reassuring to hear the sound, coming from a kind of lean-to extension immediately above the main entrance, of a toilet being flushed. But we met Andy often in the pub. During one of those visits, he related one alcoholic evening in Exeter when he and another chap, both buzzed on lager, had managed to steal a big orange glass globe from a pole at one end of a pedestrian crosswalk. These globes covered flashing lights, known as Belisha beacons, had strong appeal as trophies, but if somebody was seen by the police carrying one these things, there would be some awkward questions to answer. Maggie was with them that night, and they got the trophy home because she had stuck it under her sweater pretending to be pregnant.

We met Andy quite a few years later during a trip back to England from Canada. It was in Paddington Station, and we noticed him having a pint in one of the station pubs, so we joined him. He had flunked out of Exeter and he explained that he had found a job as a night watchman at a warehouse in Slough.

"In fact", he said, pointing to a train just leaving the station, "that's my train."

"What if the warehouse is robbed?" Maggie asked.

"Not my fault", Andy said. "I wasn't there."

I watched Maggie's expression. She might have found Andy's tossed-off remark humorous in her student days. But that afternoon, in the Paddington Station pub, her face showed concern. Andy had not been important in her life at Exeter; he had been just another irresponsible student, and there was a bit of the devil in everyone at that stage. But she was obviously disturbed that somebody she had known seemed now to be sliding into oblivion. And I have many mental images of Maggie over the years, showing her need to offer a hand, to assist others who had somehow missed the boat and who were becoming another of society's dispossessed. In later years, Maggie's natural willingness to help others remained. And there were situations when that desire and an openly expressed request for her to help came up against what seemed a learned inability of people to take responsibility for themselves. On more than one occasion, Maggie was hurt when her concern and interest in helping appeared to be rebuffed without gratitude and apparently for no good reason.

The couple who operated our pub, The Beehive, were called Julie and Danny. More than once Maggie reminded Danny gently that his outside sign hadn't been turned on. One evening, Julie quietly brought Maggie up to date on the metal bowls on the bar that held peanuts. The hairy workmen holding up the bar helped themselves to these peanuts. Julie informed Maggie that the bowls were placed on the floor during weekends as water containers for patrons' dogs. But she ensured Maggie in all seriousness that they were washed thoroughly at the end of each weekend before entering "peanut" service on the bar during the week. Maggie treated the peanuts in those bowls ever after as though they were tainted.

Maggie remained at Aslib. She loved the work, she was fond of most of her colleagues, and she was developing formidable skills that she would apply to great effect throughout her career. I had begun sending in resumes in response to ads, and with one of these I struck pay dirt. I was interviewed twice, offered the job, I accepted, and that led to another chapter in my life with Maggie.

CHAPTER 6

DRUGS AND A CATHEDRAL

The job I was offered and which I accepted was as a medical representative for a company called Winthrop. That job involved making low-key sales pitches to general practitioners, visiting hospitals and getting to know the doctors at various levels, and checking at pharmacies to determine whether they were having any problems acquiring either the over-the-counter or ethical products that Winthrop produced. The focus of this activity was not actually to sell anything, but to keep the company's profile as visible as possible and to leave product information and samples with doctors.

To equip me for this activity, I attended a month-long training course at a rather posh pub in Weybridge. I was one of approximately fifteen trainees, the rest of whom came from all across the UK. They were a most interesting group, all male, and I got to know some of them quite well.

During the week we all lived, dual occupancy, at the pub, which had about twenty guest rooms. Classes were from nine to five, and in those classes we were taught some anatomy, some biology, some biochemistry, and a lot about the drugs the company produced. We practised "sales techniques" or how to talk to busy doctors who really wanted to see patients, not salesmen. We each picked up a company car early in the training course, and we could use those cars to travel to wherever home was on weekends. Even though we students turned the classes into raucous, raunchy affairs, we all learned a great deal, perhaps even *because* there was so much backchat. If the days were raucous, the evenings were much more so.

Early in the course, it was discovered that I knew virtually no rugby songs, and this struck my course mates as an incomprehensible and shocking lacuna. One of the Welsh trainees took me in hand, and within a few days, I had mastered about a dozen coarse rugby songs, long before political rectitude had been dreamt of. My Welsh "instructor" was delighted by my progress, and I was accepted as a successfully reconstructed outcast. I was in regular telephone contact, two or three times a week, with Maggie, who had moved from New Cross to occupy Jessica Road full time. I related to her my rugby songs adventure with some pride. Having her student days only recently behind her, she was pleased, shall we say, that I had become more like the rough-edged degenerates she had known at Exeter, even though she felt obliged to lament my clear deviation from full respectability. I went back to Jessica Road every weekend, and face-to-face discussion confirmed that she was ambivalent about my transformation into one of the "lads". But she was delighted at this development in my working life. I was on the way to doing actual work at a job that required me to wear a good suit, that would bring in much more cash, and that came with a car.

Looking back, this marked the beginning of a period when Maggie's life and mine were settling into something having a solid basis. By this time, I had no doubt that Maggie was the one for me, and that I would ask her to marry me. But there were still big changes afoot affecting how much time we would be able to spend together. The major one involved the "patch" where I would be functioning as a medical rep. Toward the middle of the training course, I was informed that my patch would be a sprawling area that stretched across the middle of Southern England, and included part of Hampshire, most of Wiltshire, part of Dorset, and a small piece of Somerset. This was mostly rural, meaning that it would be hard work seeing my quota of doctors each day. Every day's visits had to be planned carefully to group together enough doctors whose surgeries (what doctors' offices are referred to in Britain) were sufficiently close to one another. There were several hundred GPs in my patch, five or six hospitals, and many pharmacies. I would be expected to see at least four doctors a day. This meant that I had to be waiting to see the first doctor before any patients arrived, give him or her my pitch as quickly as was polite, and go like the wind to the next doctor on the list. Visiting the third, fourth, and fifth doctors likely would mean waiting my turn among those doctors' morning patients. Most doctors' surgeries closed before noon.

During the second last week of my training course, Maggie and I consulted a map on Friday evening after I had returned to London to see where I might establish myself within my patch. My home base needed to be reasonably central and as close to the larger towns as possible. It proved impossible to meet all the requirements, to find a location that was best without any doubt. Best, that is, from a work perspective. Finally, we decided that the best choice was Salisbury. So, that weekend, we drove to Salisbury on Saturday morning. We bought a local paper and began hunting for places to rent.

There weren't a lot, and in fact we identified only two that looked plausible. Maggie was quite excited about Salisbury but was aware that it might be necessary to look elsewhere if I could find nothing suitable in this distinguished cathedral city. The second of the two advertisements we had marked was a house in a small lane called Ayleswade Road. One approached the house along a gravel drive off Ayleswade Road, the drive being overhung by trees. The property had evidently been somewhat neglected, but it happened that the neglect turned out to have a benign face. The front door was almost completely obscured by overgrown trees and shrubs, but this gave the place the appearance of some imaginary spot in English literature.

There were three young men sharing the house, themselves all in sales as well, and the ad had been placed by one of them, Gerry. Gerry was very welcoming. He showed us around the house, on two levels. The kitchen was at the back of the house, and from the kitchen window one looked across fields, across the river Avon, and there was the spire of the cathedral. Having had the tour, Maggie and I went outside to confer. It was a short conference. Maggie said simply, "Yes, please!" through a bright smile. So the deal was inked, my settling-in date was agreed, and Maggie was delighted. One other benefit emerged from all this. Gerry became a close and lifelong friend to both of us.

So I established myself in Salisbury and began working as a medical rep. The work was gruelling: studying road maps and my lists of doctors every evening, planning each morning's work, trying to see my daily quota of doctors, driving like the wind through the countryside. I often didn't make my quota. But there was something else that the company relied on quite heavily, and they called it "memorability". I and the other reps had to submit details of which doctors we saw on which days, and the company would follow up by asking samples of the doctors whether they remembered our visits. I had something of an advantage here, since as soon as I began speaking many of my doctors suddenly were paying attention. *What's a North American doing here?* I could see them asking themselves. I began talking about Canada whenever I could. One doctor was a keen fisherman and we spoke about salmon fishing on the Miramichi. Another doctor was curious about winter, and I told him about gangs of snowploughs clearing long, straight, flat stretches of highway in Manitoba. A third doctor was keen on agriculture, and we drifted into a discussion about endless fields in Saskatchewan where wheat waved in the moonlight. My memorability was off the charts. I was asked how I did it. I just mumbled something about a magnetic personality or some other throw-away comment.

I told Maggie about all this and she thought it was hilarious. "Leave it to you to become a big-time fibber", but she also thought that the doctors would remember the company I represented. Maggie was a believer in good advertising, and a proponent of the "if it works use it" school.

Maggie came to Salisbury at least one weekend a month. We wandered the city, which was then a rather down-at-heel market town on the edge of Salisbury Plain. Many years later, we visited the city again and found it much gentrified.

But my experiences inside and outside the city were quite different. There were military camps in the countryside all around Salisbury, and I recounted to Maggie how, on several occasions, I had been driving along a highway and had a tank suddenly lurch across the road in front of me. The military presence in Salisbury itself was unavoidable, since off-duty soldiers went there for pub evenings. Most of these chaps, and they were virtually all men in those days, were decent conversable sorts. One of the things that Maggie noticed right away was that Salisbury had an astonishing number of pubs for a city its size.

Another thing that poked through almost everywhere in and around Salisbury was history. Remnants of Roman roads trace across the countryside, and with the help of some books from the Salisbury Public Library, I found and walked a few of these. Maggie became interested in this right away and wanted the full story on my Roman ramblings, with pictures if possible. One of these old Roman roads leads to an immense ruin called Calleva Atrebatum near the village of Silchester, not far from Basingstoke. It is basically the site of a large walled Roman military city. Just north of Salisbury is Old Sarum, a hill fort going way back, which was the site of a Norman cathedral, to which the current cathedral in central Salisbury is the successor. As has been the case for most of the places I have lived, I regret not spending more time exploring the many aspects of Salisbury's long history.

Maggie and I visited Salisbury Cathedral many times. It is possibly the most elegant of all the English cathedrals and is displayed in a large cathedral close, surrounded by acres of grass. We went to the cathedral a number of times to hear choral evenings, and for a couple of organ concerts. I can remember clearly the look on Maggie's face on those occasions. This was deep English culture and history, in a building almost eight hundred years old, and she fit in and felt right at home with it. We spent a half day at Stonehenge just north of Salisbury, and the power of the place had a clear effect on Maggie, something that once again I could see in her face. There is a small village called Pitton a few miles from Salisbury, and there was a delightful pub there called The Silver Plough. The inside of the pub was all low dark beams, and there were horse brasses everywhere. Often when I asked Maggie where she would like to go for a pint, she would say without hesitation, "The Silver Plough". A small pub within walking distance of Ayleswade Road was The Victoria and Albert. Maggie and I were there one night during a 1972 miners' strike, when there were rotating power blackouts. Staff at The Victoria and Albert rose to the challenge without blinking an eye; the whole pub was illuminated by dozens of candles. It was almost magical. Maggie's eyes glowed. At times like those, I was reassured that in deciding "not to let this one get away" I had made the right decision.

Something that was common back then in many areas of England was a characteristic odour in the air in autumn and winter. It was the smell of coal smoke. Many people used coal fires, possibly as much for atmosphere as for warmth. Maggie was used to the odour, took it for granted. It was me who stopped dead when I smelled it, sniffed the air, and said how strongly it spoke to me. I'm almost certain that this odour had such an impact because it brought back childhood memories of watching the great black iron horses huff their way into and out of my home village in Ontario. Soon, Maggie was also sniffing the air and would break into a suppressed laugh when I looked at her knowingly.

About once a month I would travel to London for the weekend, and Maggie and I would snuggle down in Jessica Road. It felt like coming home, and it felt like that because Maggie was there.

In many ways, life was simple, and perhaps because of that, the enjoyment of simple things meant a great deal. We took regular walks through the neighbourhood. Fish and chips, fish fingers, and eggs on cheese on toast were quite acceptable as main meals. A game of Halma in the evening was common. Maggie continued to work at Aslib and continued to love what she did. She got along particularly well with several colleagues. We were all in our midtwenties. One of those colleagues was single and a highly intelligent, quirky woman, having a wicked sense of badinage and enjoyment. We spent some time with Ruth, but I had the impression also that for much of the time she was a cat who walked by herself. All but one of Maggie's colleagues were women. The sole male was known as "Fingers" and he always rode the elevator alone. One of Maggie's colleagues, Jenny, was married, and the four of us would have pub nights. One Friday night when I arrived late at Jessica Road, Maggie came running down the stairs when she heard me enter, tried to tell me a story, but kept bursting into laughter. It involved Jenny. This young woman had come home from work one evening and was looking forward to the arrival of her husband. Apparently, they usually arrived home at about the same time. She thought she would give him a surprise, so she took off all her clothes and lay spread-eagle on the bed. Time passed. No husband. She began to get chilly, but reasoned, *Any time now...* About an hour later than expected, the husband blew in, the victim of some commuter train snarl up. Maggie broke out laughing again when she related her colleague's order to her husband. "Quick! I'm freezing! Come and warm me up!"

Another colleague at Aslib was a tall Australian woman named Peta, and she and Maggie slid into an easy friendship. We went with her to pub nights in Earl's Court, then known as Kangaroo Court. We saw *The Adventures of Barry McKenzie* with her and a flock of Australians, and I'm sure we laughed more at the backchat than at the film. That Australian friend left Aslib, changed boats completely, and went to work in a mathematics centre in Amsterdam, where she stayed for about twelve years. She then changed boats again, took up the study of academic philosophy, surfaced at McGill University in Montreal for her doctorate, then went back to Australia where she joined the teaching staff at Murdoch University in Perth. While she was at McGill she visited Toronto several times. On one of those occasions we took her to Niagara Falls, which she had never seen. Peta and Maggie looked like the antithesis of each other: one tall, lanky, and loping, the other short and bouncy. I can remember them walking through the heavy mist sweeping in from the falls, deep in animated conversation, me following behind and wondering about this unlikely pair. Peta was overcome by the sight of the waterfalls, dropped into broad Australian in her excitement, and had Maggie falling down laughing when she declared that she had never seen "so much woddah in me loif".

Now to step back a year or so in this narrative. As Christmas loomed in 1971, Maggie said to her mother that she suspected the Canadian had nowhere to go at Christmas, and could she bring him to Stroud. I found out about this after it was all settled, but indeed I had begun wondering what I would do at Christmas. I went off to Stroud with Maggie, flattered but not really knowing what to expect, although sensing that some threshold had been crossed. Maggie's family couldn't have been more welcoming, but I found out later that one question burned in their minds: Would the Canadian fit into the Walker Christmas traditions? It turned out that this was important. At least one other young man who had turned up at Sandpipers for parental scrutiny hadn't passed muster.

I was introduced to a good number of these traditions. One was that, in one's Christmas stocking, there would always be something edible, and the recipient was expected to eat it or at least try it. Maggie's mother had put into my stocking a jar of large Polish dill pickles. I smiled at it, opened the jar, pulled out a pickle, and ate it. There was applause all round, but I held up a hand. I pulled out all the other pickles, one at a time, and ate them.

There were Christmas family games in front of the fireplace. One of these was called "I packed my bag and in it I put…" And in that game one person started by saying what they put in the bag. It then went to the next person who said what they put in the bag. But the trick here was that before you said what else you were going to put in the bag, you had to recite all the things that already had been placed in it by everyone else. The contents were the most outrageous mix of things, such as a tin of bloater paste, a box of thumbtacks (which are called drawing pins in England), a half hundredweight of Andrews liver salts, and in fact anything from the mundane to the outlandish. And the game would carry on until the bag had dozens of items in it. The humour and the excitement came at being able to catch someone when it was their turn and their recital missed an item or got them in the wrong order. When I was younger, I had a very good memory, and I became a star at this game. Many years later, I was able to astonish Maggie and her family by being able to remember the first four items chosen in that first game: a lump of coal, a raisin, a tooth-brush, a comb. Maggie's mother told me at one point that Maggie had mentioned repeatedly that episode of "I packed my bag". The family warmth and the generous welcome I received that first Christmas was doubtless what made everything so memorable.

There was music — Maggie's father playing the piano, something he excelled at — and everyone singing. We sang carols, folk songs, a few bawdy songs, and songs that Tom Lehrer and Flanders and Swann had made well known. There was a crossword-puzzle exercise, in which somebody entered a word then passed the puzzle to the next person who had to enter another word, and so it went around the group. I was no good at this, although over the years, with Maggie's help, I gained some ability at English crosswords. Maggie's mother seemed to see something in me, and we became fairly close over just a short year. In the early months, she never asked what the future held for Maggie and me, but I'm sure she guessed where we were headed.

We moved into the new year, and as the months went by, I confided in Maggie that a medical rep's job wasn't what I was cut out for. Maggie's response was simple and to the point: "So look for something else." I had come to the same conclusion and that's what I had begun doing. During my job searching, there was a period of time when my activities were clearly entertaining for Maggie. I would take some time off in order to attend interviews for jobs. The interviews could be anywhere, and when an interview finished, I would phone home (there was a pay telephone on the tenants' landing, or I was told to feel free to call the landlady's number) to tell Maggie where I was and when I would be back in London. Once I called from Newcastle. Another time I called from Leicester. I called from Birmingham, from Bristol, from Southampton. Eventually I did land a new job — in London. It was then late spring of 1972.

And once again, things changed for me — and more importantly, for Maggie and me.

CHAPTER 7

A WINDY NIGHT TO REMEMBER

Once I moved back to London to start my new job, Maggie's life and mine, from day to day, came more into sync. My new job was in Theobalds Road, not far from the British Museum, while Maggie continued at Aslib. In my new work, I was back into things technical, splitting my time as an author and a reviewer of abstracts that summarized the essential elements in newly issued patents. This work meant also that Maggie's and my fields of endeavour had moved closer together. Maggie often had to deal with patent information, and in fact she considered anything related to information to be in her viewfinder. So now we had more things to discuss — and sometimes to disagree on.

As we both were working in Central London, our mornings were also very much in sync. Breakfast was usually coffee and toast, and no morning was complete without a dose of Tony Blackburn on BBC Radio 1. We always tuned in to BBC Radio 1 on Saturdays when we were in London, to listen to Noel Edmonds. Since both of us were reading things all day and every day, we seldom looked at newspapers, apart from the *Sunday Telegraph* and Sunday *Observer*. Having done breakfast, we would leave Jessica Road together, make our way — on foot or by bus if a handy one came along — to Clapham Junction, where we would catch a commuter train to Victoria Station. From Victoria, Maggie would walk along Upper Belgrave Street to Belgrave Square where Aslib was located. From Victoria I would catch the Number 38 bus, which eventually dropped me about fifty metres from where I worked. In the evening, we would arrive home at roughly the same time.

During this phase of our life together, our income was reasonable, if not lavish, for people our age. We had modest expenses. We owned no property. I no longer had any of the costs of running a car. And so for people of our age and status, we lived well. But despite our relative affluence, I was intrigued and charmed, by turns, at the frugal habits Maggie retained.

In those days, we got green stamps with food purchases in some supermarkets. We could stick these stamps into booklets and they could then be redeemed for modest discounts. Maggie followed this practice unfailingly, and she probably saved us several hundred pounds over the years. She also made good use of luncheon vouchers.

Luncheon vouchers were a big thing then. Maggie received a certain fixed number per week, I don't remember exactly how many. If I recall correctly, they were worth 15p each, and she would stop at a small hole-in-the-wall place somewhere along Upper Belgrave Street and get two bread rolls filled with cream cheese. I tended to turn up my nose at luncheon vouchers, perhaps because they weren't handed out by my employer, more likely because I was just a bit full of myself.

My days with Maggie were all special, but Tuesdays were special for a different reason. That was the day the weekly issue of *New Scientist* appeared, and we would pick up a copy at the WH Smith newsstand in Victoria Station. Although not trained in any science, Maggie could understand anything presented in plain language, she had a keen sense of what was important and what was interesting, and she was unfailingly curious about almost everything around her. As a result, she always read *New Scientist* from cover to cover. In a project she undertook as part of post-graduate studies that she would sign up for later, she produced a credible summary of the information available on black holes. Maggie's information on these then mysterious celestial objects all came from issues of *New Scientist*.

We were now spending a lot more time together, and we were learning about what it meant to live as a couple. We hit surprisingly few bumps in the road, although there were some, and one or two of them were nasty jolts. It was at about this time that the other tenant in 14 Jessica Road, a large, gentle, teddy bear of a man from Northern Ireland, moved out, and the landlady asked if we wanted to rent both rooms. His room was more spacious than ours, and it faced south onto Jessica Road and had two lovely bay windows. We leapt at the chance, and we then had what was almost a true self-contained flat: two rooms and our own kitchen. Having advanced more toward a "home" than just having a "bedsit", Maggie started a herb garden in window boxes on the outside window sills in our "new" room, and it worked fairly well. There was one sparrow, however, who took an inexplicable liking to thyme, and it would pull up the thyme plants as fast as Maggie replaced them. It was a war of wills, but one where the sparrow eventually claimed victory when Maggie, uncharacteristically, threw in the towel.

During 1972 and into 1973, our social life expanded considerably. This was partly because we both worked with interesting groups of people and we began to socialize with them. There was a very enjoyable weekend in Kent with one of my work colleagues, more boozy evenings at Kangaroo Court, and invitations to the homes of people I worked with, all of them in London. We also made several treks to my cousin's place in Harrow, where I had stayed for a few days during my first trip to England in 1970.

Maggie came across more of her old Exeter contacts who had gravitated to London. One of them lived in a flat in Islington and operated what he called "the magic saucepan". On Monday, he would open a tin of something, pour it into the saucepan, and eat some of it for dinner. The next day he would open another tin of something (it didn't seem to matter what), add it to the saucepan, and have some for dinner. This continued through the week. Maggie found out about this and insisted on going to his flat during the weekend, emptying what was left in the saucepan, and scrubbing it thoroughly so that nothing could fester for more than five or six days. He was one of a group of chaps at Exeter for whom Maggie agreed to go to their student flat and prepare dinner on Saturdays. The catch was that there was only a half hour window for eating, the half hour that fell between two television programmes, *Match of the Day* and *Doctor Who*. Maggie always maintained that that was the best training she could have had for cooking to a schedule. Having met Magic Saucepan and a few of Maggie's other fellow Exeter students, it was obvious that Maggie stood out in several ways. Although she thoroughly enjoyed bouts of ribald conversation, she also insisted on intelligent discussion. She was equally at home speaking to women or men. She would never simper when talking to men, she would just walk away from insecure macho types, and she was turned off completely by mincing "girlie" behaviour on the part of women. For Maggie, people were people first and women and men after that. Though, having said that, Maggie was very sensitive to the different vulnerabilities of men and women in general and was sympathetic to particular problems faced by individual men and women.

One evening when we were at home in Jessica Road, Maggie asked me about insecurity. I said I wasn't sure what she was getting at. She then said that she had wondered sometimes whether it was harder for a girl to become a woman or a boy to become a man. "Not physically, I mean", she said. "That just happens. I mean men being comfortable doing what men do, and women being comfortable doing what women do." We talked about it for a while. Then Maggie wondered about the difference between the feelings a man might have in suggesting something to a woman and being refused, and a woman waiting for a man to suggest something and worrying that it might never happen. I have not found this awareness in that many other people, but for Maggie it seemed to be an essential part of the warp and weft of who she was.

During the summer of 1972, Maggie took some time to go back to Stroud and spend it with her parents. While she was away, I went for a long walk one mild and windy night. The trees on Wandsworth Common caught the wind and made big gestures to the sky. I began that walk in a state of turmoil. What was I doing? Where was my life going? I must have walked for more than an hour. I came to the realization that there was only one path forward that made any sense, and that I would not be walking that path alone. I came to a decision that night, and the trees suddenly seemed to be waving their branches in approval. The next day, I phoned Maggie and asked her to meet me in Oxford, and there, in the University Parks, I proposed to her. She said later that it didn't come as a surprise.

It became known among Maggie's family and her family's friends that we were now definitely an item, and I think that resulted in some further social occasions. That seemed to be the case one afternoon when long-standing friends of Joan and John called on us unexpectedly in Jessica Road, saying that they happened to be in London and had some time free. Maggie answered the door, led our guests upstairs, and made frantic behind-the-back hand signals to me to turn over the tablecloth to hide the stains. I did, only to find that we had already turned it over once. We pleaded poverty and overwork. They looked at our brick-and-plank bookshelves and laughed indulgently. We had another very enjoyable trip to a lovely spot in Essex, a village called Layer de la Haye, not far from Colchester. During that trip, I had to be dragged away from the historical aspects of Colchester, Maggie decided definitively that she had eaten her last raw oyster, and we attended a party where the dozens of balloons covering the walls were inflated condoms that the host and hostess had brought back from a recent two-year sojourn in the Philippines. The reliability of Filipino condoms was demonstrated when all the balloons deflated less than an hour into the evening. On that occasion, Maggie wore her hair in bunches, one bunch on each side of her head. At that point, her chronological age was twenty-two, but her petite size, her youthful face, and the way she wore her hair made her look about fifteen. I clearly recall receiving looks from many of the other young men about my age, looks that were envious or accusatory or some combination, and I'm sure that more than a few of them thought, *You jammy bastard!* But the responses of those young men were based on more than just some absurd cradle-robbing fantasy. Maggie always had a friendly and open face and immense human appeal, and although she was obviously attractive as a young woman and was completely comfortable in a woman's skin, she wanted to be seen as a person above all else and always felt impatient if she sensed she was being viewed as any sort of sex object or eye candy. I always felt that those characteristics were obvious in Maggie and that they made her attractive as a person, above all else.

There was another event in 1973 that put a different spin on things for us. In May of that year, we travelled to Toronto and were married. It proved difficult to make the necessary arrangements from London for a city-hall ceremony in Toronto, so I had to scramble when we arrived. The whole business was frustrating but it did mean that, out of necessity, our wedding was a simple affair. It turned out that there were no time slots available at city hall for a civil wedding, and we found a kindly pastor in a small outpost of the African Episcopalian Methodist Church. The pastor, Reverend Estabrook, was very kind. Maggie wore a gorgeous reddish-brown suit that she had made, and there were just a handful of people present: my best man, my mother, and two good friends. Afterward, we all went to Ed's Warehouse, my mother's favourite dining spot in Toronto, for a wedding feast.

There were two main reasons why we travelled to Toronto to be married. One was that Maggie wanted my mother to be present at the marriage of her firstborn. This was typical of Maggie. Even for something as important as her own wedding, she was putting someone else's considerations ahead of her own. The second was that, just the previous year, Maggie's twin brother Chris had been married. It was a sumptuous wedding in Stroud, and Maggie was concerned about her parents being subjected to two formal weddings so quickly, one after the other. I talked to Maggie about this and we came up with a plan.

I approached Maggie's father.

"You're probably aware, John, that Maggie and I will be married at some point."

My future father-in-law looked at me noncommittally.

"We're going to elope", I said.

"Well, hang on! I'm not supposed to know that you're going to elope!" he said, a statement expressed in some puzzlement.

"True, in general. But this won't be a normal elopement."

John was quick on the uptake, and it took him no time to realize that he was being invited to participate in this little jape. He smiled and said that he supposed there was some planning to do.

In a way, we did elope when we boarded the plane for Toronto unmarried, intending to return married. But it was the "elopement ceremony" back in England that touched everyone's funny bone. John wrote me a £50 "elopement" cheque. He and I placed a ladder up to the window of Maggie's bedroom in the cottage in Westrip, Maggie climbed the ladder, despite her dislike of heights, and a few "elopement pictures" were taken. Unfortunately, I never did receive copies of those pictures, and I have been unable to find them during the decades since. Perhaps it is intended that any evidence of an elopement should be suppressed. After this "elopement ceremony", the four of us had lunch in the garden, with champagne. I think that, in a way, the whole thing was as memorable for my parents-in-law as a more formal wedding. It certainly was a low-stress affair. And it turned out that Joan and John had something else up their sleeve anyway.

People have reacted in strange ways to the story of our wedding. Some said that Maggie and I missed an important rite of passage, that it all sounded cheap and grubby, that I cheated Maggie out of what should have been one of her life's great moments. Both Maggie and I rejected comments like these vigorously. Our wedding was entirely meaningful to us. We spoke the same vows. We signed the same paperwork. We wouldn't have felt any more married if we had had a big showy affair with dozens of guests. After our marriage in Toronto, we flew to Vancouver, spent time with friends there, then enjoyed a week on the Sechelt Peninsula at the home of a friend of Maggie's mother, Katie, and her amazing husband, Paul, an Austrian who had narrowly escaped Hitler's war machine. Paul was something of an audiophile, and we listened to recordings of Jussi Björling and Robert Merrill singing "The Pearl Fishers Duet", university drinking songs sung by the Viennese opera singer Erich Kunz, and recordings of the bells in Cologne Cathedral. We watched eagles. We observed orcas swimming in the Strait of Georgia between the mainland and Vancouver Island. We helped Paul barbecue fresh Pacific salmon. We had some of Paul's choice wines. We sat around talking about love and life. And Maggie and I went for long walks along the seashore. As a honeymoon, it hit all the right buttons. Neither of us would have wanted anything else.

From Vancouver we returned to Toronto and were feted by friends and relatives. Then we returned to London. The overnight flight back, as a flight, was as memorable (or unmemorable) as it ever is. But once morning had broken and we were over England, things became more interesting. We had seats on the port side of the plane, and Maggie had a window seat.

"There's the Bristol Channel", she said.

"Can you see the Stroud Valleys?" I asked.

"No. But look! Down there!"

I looked. Roads converged on a point, like spokes of a wheel, and it was almost certain that they once had been Roman roads.

"What's the town?" I asked.

"I think it's Cirencester!" Maggie exclaimed, as though she was recognizing it for the first time.

Haze and cloud intervened shortly after that, and we glided toward Heathrow.

A few hours later, we were back in Jessica Road. It was a Wednesday, and we had organized with our places of work to take the next two days off. A small pile of mail awaited us. There were three cards from people who obviously had heard about our elopement. There was also a card from Maggie's parents. It was an invitation to attend a wedding feast that weekend at their cottage. Our wedding feast.

"Did you know about this?" I asked, feeling both surprised and flattered.

"No", Maggie said. "No idea what they're doing."

We telephoned Maggie's parents and said we would arrive on the usual 18:15 train from Paddington two days hence.

After that, we realized just how beat we were, jet lagged, but still glowing from a week by the Pacific. A meaningful glance was all it took, and we slid into our own bed for a midday nap, the first time back at home in London as a married couple.

The wedding feast was quite an affair. Joan and John had erected a marquee on their lawn. They had invited about fifty people, including all Maggie's small extended family, and many of their own friends and neighbours. Tables under the marquee were laden with salads, vegetables and dips, cold meats, finger foods of all sorts, many desserts, fruit juices, soft drinks, and a more than ample supply of wine. Maggie and I were congratulated, toasted, ribbed, and photographed, and such speeches as were made competed against a background of friendly heckling and the particular sort of ribald commentary that is often found on high-spirited occasions in England. The whole event was thoroughly relaxed and enjoyable, and looking back I don't think I would have wanted it any other way.

It was sometime after we had returned to London that Maggie signed up for a non-degree post-graduate course at City University, mainly out of interest but partly to give herself some documented training in the information work she was doing. She found the course interesting, and she threw herself into it, as she did for all her work and projects. She had convinced Aslib to give her a day off per week to attend the lectures, and on her way to the university, she walked through the Smithfield meat market.

At that time, both Maggie's and my work had revealed the need, or at least the desirability, for us to become more proficient at foreign languages. In Maggie's case, the languages were German and Russian. Mine were German and French. Compared to my English work colleagues, I already had something of a head start in French, and I found a class associated with the Goethe-Institut not far from Victoria Station, where I signed up for German conversation one evening a week. In my work, I was part of a group of people who oversaw the publication of short summaries of current patents in German, French, and English. These summaries were printed weekly in booklets by subject and sold as an alerting service that companies received on subscription. Gaining a basic grip on German through the evening class and having to wade through German patents for at least a few hours most days meant that my knowledge and ability to read German advanced very quickly. Maggie and I shared notes on how we used our newfound language skills, but our two areas of subject matter were so different in their details that not much of the vocabulary was common. Looking back, this foray into German seemed almost preordained, although we had no inkling of it at the time.

After my first Christmas at Stroud, Maggie and I travelled to her parents' place every second or third weekend, and on visits there, I was always made to feel welcome. Joan and John's house was located high up on the western slope of the valleys, and the views to the east over the Stroud Valleys are spectacular. Walking to the top of the hill behind Maggie's parents' house allowed equally gorgeous westward views over the much larger Severn Valley. I found everything about those visits civilized: the train journey and especially the more rustic section of it from Swindon to Stroud; the welcome I always received at Joan and John's home, Sandpipers, which was a delightful Cotswold cottage; the snug sitting room with fire and piano; the always interesting conversation; the appreciative if sometimes tongue-in-cheek reading of the local newspaper, the *Stroud News and Journal*, otherwise known as the Snaj; Joan's inventive cooking, an ability she certainly handed down to Maggie; and the day trips that occurred at practically every visit.

For those weekends where a trip to Stroud was planned, Maggie would order a roast of beef in the morning as she passed through

Smithfield on her way to lectures and then pick it up on her way back in the afternoon. For those weekends, at noon on Friday I would visit a quality coffee merchant called Carwardines and buy a pound of Kenyan AA coffee beans. These would be our basic contributions to the weekend. I would leave work in good time on Friday afternoon and meet Maggie at Paddington Station to catch the 18:15 train. Once out of London, the ride along the Thames Valley was something I always found otherworldly. Here was *Wind in the Willows* country. Windsor Castle was usually visible if we happened to be on the right-hand side of the carriage. The train also passed by the water meadow called Runnymede, not far from Staines and of Magna Carta fame. Sometimes one had to change trains at Swindon, and sometimes not. But from Swindon onward, I always had the feeling that we had moved more deeply into enchanted Cotswold country. Beyond Swindon, the stops were typically at Kemble, Stroud, Stonehouse, Gloucester, and Cheltenham. Also at spots beyond Swindon, there was a pronounced shift into stronger West Country accents, as the arrival of the train was announced in each station. After leaving Kemble, the train entered the Sapperton Tunnel, which cuts beneath the Cotswold Escarpment. When the train emerged from this tunnel, at Chalford, we were in the beautiful Chalford Valley, one of the five Stroud Valleys, and the magic was complete. Here, houses cling to the steep valley sides, in places steep enough that two storeys or more of a house could be against the same hillside. In spring and autumn, we would reach Chalford at twilight, and lights would twinkle up and down the valley. Because the track was more winding here, the train travelled more slowly, allowing one to take in everything. I never tired of that trip to Stroud.

A trip to Sandpipers inevitably meant an enthusiastic welcome by Maggie's parents, conversation, tours of the garden, shopping, chores, often a Saturday-night movie on television, excellent meals, and usually some excursion. I had my own chores there and they were always the same: picking snails and slugs and disposing of them, pulling wild garlic wherever I found it, trampling down the compost heap, picking brambles in season, and collecting fallen larch branches for fire kindling. There was often a trip by John, me, and Maggie's brother, Chris, if he was there, to the pub in Randwick known as the Carpenters Arms, or the Carps for short. It seemed that there was always a game of dominoes and of darts in progress in the Carps. Conversation among the locals often consisted of short declarations followed by muttered statements of agreement. Occasionally, but not very often, a serious debate would break out. When this happened, both sides would dig in, and repeated statements and repeated denials would be made until one side lost interest, and things returned to low-level murmuring. It is perhaps needless to say that my description of this lovely watering hole dates from the early 1970s, and the Carpenters Arms today is a very different place.

Excursions from Sandpipers came in many forms. Sometimes it was a trip to Gloucester Cathedral to listen to a practice of the Three Choirs in which John sang. Sometimes it was a trip to the Prinknash monastery, about halfway between Stroud and Cheltenham, to look at the gorgeous porcelain they produced there and perhaps to buy one or two pieces. Sometimes it was a trip to the mat factory, an old woollen mill next to a stream in the bottom of one of the valleys, which had been converted to making high-quality placemats. A good eye here could snag mats at low cost — the flaws making them seconds were almost invisible. Some days it was a trip to a mill that sold lengths of lovely woollen fabric. Maggie often visited the woollen mill and would purchase a few yards of beautiful material. That material would go back to London or, later, back to Toronto, where it would be placed in a trunk that contained a collection of previous purchases. The intent was to make clothes, hangings, or other things, an intent achieved only on occasion, and Maggie eventually referred to this trunk as The Albatross, a dead weight that, figuratively, she carried around her neck. Sometimes an excursion from Stroud involved a trip to Bath, an outing that was known to Joan and Maggie as a "bunbury". This was a reference to Oscar Wilde's play *The Importance of Being Earnest,* in which the character Algernon would avoid some social engagement that didn't appeal to him by diving into another activity or diversion, and he called this substitute a bunbury. Maggie loved Bath because of its exquisite Georgian architecture. Such a bunbury was an occasion to do some desultory shopping, to stroll and chat, and to have a bite to eat at some pleasant spot. A trip to Bath with Joan was always via the A38 or a set of B roads and often passed within sight of the Tyndale Monument, a tower built in honour of William Tyndale, an early translator of parts of the Bible into English.

One particular trip to Bath stuck in Maggie's memory, and she regularly repeated the event that had made it so. We had decided to have lunch in one of those department stores that maintained an eatery on the top floor. The usual sort of crowd was there — women of an uncertain age having cups of tea and a bun or biscuit or perhaps something more substantial. It was cafeteria style, where you load up a tray, slide it along to the till, and pay. On this occasion, I went through first, Joan followed me, and Maggie brought up the rear. Instead of stopping at the till, I pushed my tray through, picked it up, and began looking for a free table. The young woman on the till hadn't been expecting that.

"Sir", she said in some concern. "You need to pay."

I pointed behind me.

"It's okay", I replied. "The battle axe is paying."

Joan pushed her tray up to the till, plunked down her handbag authoritatively, and announced, "I am the battle axe."

I knew right away that Maggie and her mother both appreciated this little ploy. Joan in particular smiled at me, as though I had met some sort of Walker-family social criterion.

And it seems that I had.

There were many "events" that happened during times when I was in Stroud, too many to document comprehensively. But here are three that stick in my mind:

On one occasion, I was asked if I would like to see the Roman pavement in Woodchester. Even though I had little idea what this meant, it sounded intriguing and I said yes. Woodchester is another village in the Stroud Valleys, basically just down the hill from where Joan and John lived. Quite some time earlier, the remains of a Roman villa had been discovered there, and this had included a small courtyard or something similar. The floor of this space had been decorated in a mosaic of small pieces of coloured tiles, and this sort of construction is called a pavement. After it had been discovered, it was recognized that the coloured tiles in the pavement at Woodchester would fade through too much exposure to light, so it was covered with protective material and then a layer of soil. This soil and protective material were removed at rare intervals and the pavement made available for public viewing for a limited time. This is what I would be able to see.

I went, and it really was interesting. The image the tiler had produced was incomplete because, over the years, people had dug into this area not knowing that the pavement was there. Maggie and I examined the pavement for about twenty minutes, then left. But it was a direct physical reminder to me that the Roman past in England left many traces, and that the Romans had stamped the imprint of their culture and way of life strongly and over a large part of the country during the roughly four hundred years they were in England.

Another event was memorable for an entirely different reason. Joan had been invited to tea at Mary and Dennis Brown's home, they being the parents of Denyse who would become Maggie's sister-in-law. Joan asked Maggie and I to come along, and we did. It wasn't a formal affair, just an occasion to have something to drink, a cookie, and a chat. Maggie wore a miniskirt that wasn't particularly risqué for the time.

We were sitting sipping and munching when Dennis came into the room carrying a newspaper. Without saying a word, he unfolded the newspaper and spread the sheets over Maggie's legs, then left the room. Maggie didn't react. In fact, nobody really reacted. Maggie sat there, sheets of newspaper on her legs, sipping her drink, while the conversation continued around her. Mr. Brown never did come back into the room, and when it was time to leave, Maggie folded up the pages of newspaper, laid them on the chair, and the three of us went back out to Joan's car.

I was intrigued, to say the least, by this bit of theatre. It was a wordless piece of social commentary, a prank, an amusing item of burlesque, and a display of sang-froid in not reacting at all to something well out of the ordinary.

The third event involved a visitor from Sweden. One of John's jobs had been at a company called Sperry. He had been hired from Harwell to work at Sperry, and one of his projects there involved designing and building some device that was of interest to the military in a number of countries. One of these countries was Sweden, and during trips to Sweden on behalf of Sperry, John met and became lasting friends with a Swedish army colonel, Jan Anshelm. During one of the weekends I had come to Stroud, Jan was there visiting John and Joan as a friend. It was near Christmas, and after dinner, everyone gathered in the sitting room as usual, John began playing the piano, and Jan's strong baritone filled the room. He sang a number of pieces in Swedish, but the one I remember best was the carol "O Helga Natt". I recall thinking at the time that this was spontaneous social sophistication and homemade entertainment at the highest level.

Quite a few years later, Jan was in Toronto on business, he contacted Maggie and me, and we all went to dinner. It was a lovely evening. I recalled that night in Stroud, and Jan remembered it clearly. That was the last time we saw Jan. Maggie and I travelled to England pretty much every year while her parents were alive. We had hoped to visit Stockholm and see Jan again and his wife, Anna-Lisa, but it seemed there never was enough vacation time.

While Maggie and I lived in London, we attended virtually every Gilbert and Sullivan operetta, as performed by the incomparable D'Oyly Carte Opera Company. I had always found the G&S operettas entertaining and delightfully absurd, and we both enjoyed these performances. We saw plays from time to time, and I'm pleased to have seen Alec Guinness and Laurence Olivier perform live. We saw Monte Python in the Drury Lane Theatre, where Maggie was terrified at rising from her seat because the steeply raked balcony primed her fear of heights. At that Monty Python performance, I recall that it was almost as entertaining to watch the audience as to watch the stage. The audience reacted predictably at intermission when someone came through the aisles announcing, "Albatross! Albatross on a stick!"

Our landlady began asking us to join her for some television shows, and we saw some classic pieces of the time: *Hancock's Half Hour, The Dave Allen Show, Morecambe and Wise, The Two Ronnies*, and *Steptoe and Son*. These mean nothing to most people today, but these shows could have us rolling off our chairs.

From London we did some short-range travelling. We visited a couple who lived in Wargrave not far from Henley, the woman having been at Exeter with Maggie. We visited other friends in York, based on a similar connection. And after they were married in 1972, we visited Chris and Denyse regularly at their prefab on the Harwell site, and later at their house in Abingdon.

There were two longer-distance visits, both of which Maggie enjoyed. These were the result of invitations from fellow medical-rep trainees, in one case involving a drive to Newcastle, and in the other, a drive to Haverfordwest at the western extreme of Wales. The Newcastle trip was a boozy affair, about which I remember not much except for the heavy smell of freshly mined coal, the large and well-appointed work-ing men's clubs and their astonishing dance floors, and how much I enjoyed Newcastle Brown Ale. The visit to Haverfordwest was to attend Paul and Susan's wedding. The homily delivered by the pastor seemed to be interminable, and his voice rose and fell in Welsh cadence, at one point calling on a refiner's fire to purify something. I had trouble follow-ing all the religious references. When I felt the pew bench vibrating, I looked over at Maggie and saw that she was only barely suppressing a serious giggle. I knew right away that she had made the connection to lines in the *Messiah* that referred to a refiner's fire. That was something we laughed about on many occasions, for a long time afterward.

At the Haverfordwest event, I found that I was being watched by an older gent during the reception. He eventually approached me.

"Look you", he began in English modulated by a singsong Welsh accent. "I've been listening to you. You're not English, are you?"

"No", I said.

"You're not Scottish or Welsh?"

"No", I said. "Further west."

"Ah! You're Irish!"

"No, further west."

"Further west?" he said, his eyebrows raised in disbelief. "There isn't anything further west!"

Maggie recalled this exchange many times.

Back in London, Maggie asked me one evening whether I enjoyed working on patent abstracts. Her question made me reflect, and it was just one instance of the flashes of intuition that Maggie was capable of. In thinking about it, I found that I did enjoy having to deal with technical material, some of it quite complex. I certainly enjoyed being exposed to French and German and the feeling that my linguistic skills were perhaps better than those of many of my contemporaries. But when I thought about where it all might lead, I was less certain. I worked with people who were twenty years my senior but were doing basically the same work I did. Did I want to carry on along this path, if one could call it that?

The answer was clear enough. I had been doing this work for more than a year. Maybe it was time for a change.

Another round of job advertisements, sending off resumes, and a few interviews followed. One opportunity struck me as interesting.

It would still involve abstracts, but it was abstracts of almost everything, intended to provide an alerting service to sectors of the electricity-supply industry in England. The job would be with an organization that no longer exists, the Electricity Council. This was basically the planning and strategy wing of the electricity-supply sector, the other and much larger component being known then as the Central Electricity Generating Board, the CEGB. That job looked like a possible entry into a large technical area. I applied.

There was enough information in the job advertisement to indicate what was involved: sufficient familiarity with French and German, a technical background, the ability to write clear English prose, and some formal experience in writing or editing. I figured that I met all these criteria, but just to hedge my bets, I went searching for some recent papers in French and in German on electricity supply. There were plenty to choose from. I chose four in each language, and my perusal of them made me confident that I could handle material at that reasonably high level without much difficulty.

I was contacted for an interview, a date was arranged, and I turned up. My interviewer turned out to be the person I would work for if hired, a tall amiable man called Arthur. There were just the two of us in a small interview room, and it became apparent that Arthur was curious as to why a Canadian would apply for this job. We got through all the preliminaries quickly, then Arthur handed me two papers.

"Take a look through these papers, please. One is in German and one is in French. I'll give you ten minutes. Then I'd like you to summarize what each paper is about."

The French paper was quite easy to read, and after a few minutes I felt I could summarize it well. It was the German paper that was a surprise. It was one of the four German-language papers I had used to prepare myself two days earlier. Since I had spent some time on that paper, I needed only a few minutes to refresh my memory. Before my ten minutes had expired, I said to Arthur that I was ready. He looked up in some surprise, then asked me to go ahead, starting with the French paper. It took me about a minute to summarize it. Arthur nodded and smiled.

"And now the German paper", he said, apparently expecting it to present the stiffer challenge.

Once again, it took me only about a minute to describe the paper's content. Arthur clearly was somewhat surprised.

"That's very good", he said. "Neither the content of that paper nor the German is particularly easy."

I came clean then, admitting that I had done some homework prior to the interview, and the paper he had asked me to examine just happened to be one of the papers I had found and read a few days earlier.

I think that clinched the position for me. Arthur was impressed. He told me that someone would be in contact with me, and the interview was over. Three days later, I received a job offer.

Maggie was pleased at this development. She felt I needed to move around a reasonable amount and experience different workplaces and different supervisors. Maggie always had a very clear idea of what her profession would be; she was always interested in the information world, libraries being just one part of that — as a repository for that general entity known as information. Maggie's view here was really quite sophisticated, even when she was still in her early twenties.

I began work at the Electricity Council and found my colleagues there to be congenial. The work was interesting and more appealing than a steady diet of only patents. I very much enjoyed the more substantial material in French and German, and my mastery of technical French and German advanced considerably. In my work at the Electricity Council, I was active in areas that were closer to what Maggie was doing, and we talked a lot about our respective jobs. It always struck me, however, that Maggie was far ahead of me, often in some senses that I found it hard to pinpoint. She always seemed to know pretty much exactly what she wanted from her working life, and she appeared to find ways to move toward what she wanted. Her idea of "information" as a general concept, and how it took shape in very specific situations was in contrast to my approach to the world. I was just some sort of "technical" guy, tightening nuts and counting rivets. Maggie was looking at abstract concepts and somehow extracting from those concepts workable real-world answers to real-world questions.

From contacts through Aslib, Maggie knew a couple of the women I worked with at the Electricity Council, and she came with me one day to the office in Millbank to meet them, see where I worked, and just fill in a further bit of the information picture that was her world. Maggie wasn't as impressed as me at the subsidized bar where

Newcastle Brown was always available. On my first visit to the sub-sidized bar with Arthur, I noted that the Newcastle Brown was in clear glass bottles and expressed concern that the ale would degrade by being exposed to light. Arthur smiled and dismissed my concern, saying that the Brown didn't remain in the bottles long enough for that to happen.

So Maggie and I continued to work at our jobs, continued to enjoy our flat in Jessica Road, and continued a pleasant and relaxed social life with friends.

At that point, I had lived in England for a little more than three years. I began wondering about the longer-term future. In particular, I began wondering about a return to Canada. This resulted in a thought pattern that ultimately took Maggie and me to Canada. And it was a move that might have been the wrong one. Indeed, beginning in about the mid- to late-1980s, I frequently had serious doubts about it all. Even more, I became convinced at a late stage that, in an important way, I had led Maggie along a path that wouldn't have been her first choice.

CHAPTER 8

A DISTANT INTERLUDE

Maggie and I arrived in Canada on September 10, 1974. And we landed in the middle of a heat wave. The weather was oppressive for a few days, then it became tolerable. Maggie didn't like hot, humid weather, so this wasn't a good start. Maggie began work at an information-searching company called SVP. This was a position she had lined up in London, and so she was able to slide into a new role in Toronto within a few days of arriving.

The group Maggie worked with at SVP were almost all women and were an interesting cross section of nationalities, ages, and interests. They all got along well. Maggie and I socialized with two of these women and their partners, but we also found new connections outside Maggie's work and picked up with people I had known before leaving to go to England some years earlier. Maggie's time at SVP lasted about two years, and it became evident from her colleagues that Maggie's training in London made her one of the most valued members of that team almost immediately. It was a fee-for-service information organization, it attracted a wide variety of clients, and as a result the work was highly varied. Most days, I got a running commentary from Maggie on some of that variety. And sometimes out of that variety, there rose a challenge that was off the wall. This was the case for one particularly memorable job.

Maggie asked me if I would go into the SVP office to do a series of telephone interviews on behalf of a client. It all had to do with condoms.

The client wanted some product and market information on different sorts of condoms, and none of the women in SVP would touch that one. So they found me a desk, I read over the information request, we did some searching in various directories, and I began phoning around. I was able to get some quite detailed and "interesting" information on condom design and some "unexpected" market information the condom companies had been able to unearth. Although none of the women at SVP would ask the questions, they all wanted to listen in on the conversations I had. And they did that. All of them.

Afterward, there was some fevered follow-up.

"Do they really make condoms with something like that on the end?"

"How long did he say was the longest condom they made?"

"Flavoured? Why would they ... Oh!"

In terms of living arrangements, we had organized, in advance, temporary accommodation in the spacious apartment where my sister lived. At least it was spacious compared to what we were used to. Within a short time, we had moved to our own rented apartment on Spadina Road near the intersection with Lonsdale. This was an odd little one-bedroom affair in an old building that seemed to have walls whose thickness was inspired by the design of a Norman castle. All the rooms were small, but it was affordable and everything worked. The superintendent, Mrs. Ritchie, was pleasant but not someone to put up with nonsense from any of her tenants. Nonsense meant leaving any sort of mess in the corridors, giving any reason for the police to come calling, and worst of all, in her eyes, making excessive noise anywhere in the building. We paid the rent for the year up front, and I remember hesitating to write a cheque for the massive sum of $1,400.

Having our own space made a difference, but the time it was taking me to find a suitable job was something that made me nervous.

I was able to pick up odd bits of low-level work that paid poorly, but at least they brought in some money and didn't interfere with my job searching. Eventually, I did find a position at Atomic Energy of Canada Limited (AECL), and that eased things considerably.

The little apartment on Spadina Road was definitely a starter, and from there we moved a year later to another rental apartment on Bloor Street just west of High Park Avenue. The disadvantages of this second location were that it was on Bloor Street, one of the city's busiest thoroughfares, it was next to a fire station, and we found out soon enough that, for various reasons, it wasn't great value. There were things in the apartment that didn't work and we couldn't get the superintendent to fix them. And what was more disquieting than disadvantageous, there was something about the superintendent that I didn't like at all. The advantages of the place were that an entrance to High Park subway station was just around the corner, we had a larger living space, the windows let in a good deal of light, and we were directly across Bloor Street from the extensive open space of High Park. It was also close to a decent supermarket and a fifteen-minute walk to my Aunt Elinor's place on Willard Avenue. I introduced Maggie to my aunt and they hit it off immediately. It was at this time that we acquired our first two cats, Rembrandt and Rubens, and having cats who greeted us in the evening when we came through the door made our place feel more like home immediately.

Our rental agreement for the place on Bloor Street was also for one year. As that rental agreement approached its end, we began looking and soon we moved again. This time, we found a place that was more congenial. It was a two-storey detached house on Galley Avenue, which was close to the east side of High Park rather than our previous location on the north side of the park. So we didn't move far, but the new neighbourhood and our landlady were both a step up. We occupied the ground floor, the landlady lived upstairs, and we had separate entrances.

We had bought a car, the cheapest new car we could find, a Mini. Its colour was given as flame red, and the tag on the key had space only to call it "f-red". So our first car was named Fred. After a few months, I noticed that Fred had developed "freckles" all along the front part of the hood. I attributed that to stone chips thrown up by vehicles in front of us, and Fred's low-slung design allowing these stone chips to knock off little flecks of red paint. Maggie had the answer right away. Although she never used nail polish ("I hate the smell of acetone and the polish makes my fingers feel hot"), she used a bottle of red nail polish she had been given to "touch up" Fred's freckles.

One day, Maggie came home and announced that she had been headhunted. A local branch of one of the big management consulting companies had called SVP as a client and asked for a "consultation" in the client's office. Maggie went and found that she was being sounded out about working in a management consulting context. They had been impressed by work that Maggie had done for them in SVP and said that their experience files needed a complete overhaul. Those files consisted of abstracts of the reports on all the consulting assignments the company had completed. The idea was to make these experience files more consistent and easier to search. When bidding on a new project, the company wanted to showcase everything they had done in the past that was relevant, and they wanted all that to be in the experience files. Because project reports were prepared by different consultants, none of whom would pick up the Nobel Prize for literature (or even a citation for clarity or conciseness), trolling in the experience files as they existed at the time was likely to yield a thin, mixed, or not very useful catch.

The possibility had immediate appeal for Maggie. It was outside any of her experience. She was intrigued, although she wasn't at all sure that it had any future. I intervened, hoping to cut through any dilemma.

"Take it", I advised.

A week later, having resigned from SVP and signed on with the consulting crowd, Maggie had a small office and a filing cabinet, and she had met some consultants whose work and personalities interested her, many of whom became friends. Within three months, Maggie had made sense of the project, had come up with search categories that her boss agreed would be immediately workable, and had converted about a third of the abstracts from opaque to intelligible English by going back to the original reports, figuring out just what had been done, and clearing those abstracts of their thick literary fog.

Within six months, the heavy lifting on the project had been done, and the work that remained was little more than maintenance. A full-time person was no longer warranted, and it looked like Maggie had done herself out of a job. Maggie's boss had noticed this change in workload and asked if she would be interested in participating in some of the projects themselves as an associate consultant. Maggie leapt at the chance.

Maggie took to consulting like a fish to water. It was in this consulting firm that she took her next level of working-world lessons. This involved understanding and navigating the politics of dealing with clients; parrying the moves of more senior consultants who fancied their chances with her; and realizing that the clarity and appeal of her writing were clear advantages. All this caught the eye of more than one partner. Maggie forged professional friendships with senior consultants that lasted for decades. Her animated presentations won a number of contracts and convinced clients to sign off on projects completed. Some of Maggie's colleagues and a few partners worried about her apparent tendency to shoot from the hip. But she was young, energetic, and soon became known as someone whose sometimes unorthodox sense of humour never failed to click. Clients picked up on this. They appreciated the directness and the urbanity. There were late nights. There were more than a few projects where she had to bone up from a standing start on new industries and new types of problems. Maggie learned that the key to many consulting contracts had more to do with people than with technical problems, and her natural human appeal but also her ability to master a new area quickly were certainly things that helped her move ahead.

The consultants had favourite watering holes — The Duke of York on Prince Arthur; The Taco Belle, a place that ceased to exist long ago; and The Whistling Oyster, now also in the past — and Maggie often invited me to join her and her consultants after work for some steam relief. They were a group who worked hard but also played hard, according to the time-worn adage, but for some staff, there was a cost. In the wake of that frenetic activity, there was the wreckage of a few marriages. Maggie worked with many people who had great personal appeal, and we mixed socially with some of them for quite a few years. That phase of Maggie's career came to an end through an unexpected opportunity, and once again, it was something that could be pinned on me. Or perhaps I should say that Maggie deferred to an opportunity that presented itself to me, but an opportunity that ultimately became ours to share.

Maggie's move from SVP to a position in the management consulting firm had made it feel as though our lives were taking root. We didn't know it then, but there were bigger changes ahead.

We were happy in Galley Avenue. In the lead up to our first Christmas there, Maggie received a Christmas card from an acquaintance of her Exeter University days, who was then living in London. And he had noticed something extraordinary. Just down Galley Avenue from us, only six or eight doors away, was another Exeter graduate, John Lockett, who Maggie had known at university, but someone she had also known from early primary-school days in England. I was out of town, I don't remember where or why, but when I arrived home fairly late that night, Maggie was dancing around excitedly, bursting to share this news but for hours having had nobody to share it with. It was only a few days later that we welcomed John and his wife, Christine, to our place for a drink. I remember that evening clearly. Our flat was comfortable and welcoming. I watched Christine and John look around, seeing what they evidently felt was a home. It was the first time I had met them, but before we finished our first glass of wine, we were all relaxed. That evening, they looked around at intervals, and what they saw caused the attributes of the idea "home" to be written across their faces. Galley Avenue was indeed the first place Maggie and I would consider "home", and the idea and the reality of "home" never left us after that. Christine and John quickly became friends and are good friends to this day.

And so Maggie and I settled into our new "home". We began entertaining in a modest way. We were relaxing into a way of life, and for both of us, our jobs were places where we felt increasingly comfortable. Maggie had really begun to hit her stride in the management consulting firm. It was the heyday for consultants. Company profits were large. Partnership commissions, the bonus payments that partners and employees received at year-end, were generous, to say the least. Maggie brought home some enthusiastic commentary on her work almost every day. I was still working in the Public Relations department at AECL, where my technical background was called upon regularly, but I was becoming less comfortable with what I felt were the glib aspects of public relations. Although I felt that a change was needed, and I talked things over with Maggie, there was no screaming urgency, so I was okay just letting the situation ride for a while. But behind all this — though I wasn't aware of it at the time — our lives were beginning to become more complex. Both our jobs came with increasing amounts of responsibility, and we were required to apply more judgment and initiative. We were no longer living the carefree footloose life we had in London.

Other things were happening, things that tended to expand our world without us fully realizing it.

Maggie and I had bought bicycles. At weekends, we went for leisurely rides. Maggie wasn't particularly keen on bicycles, because she had had to use one to get around in Stroud — to go to school, for example — and cycling in hilly country can be tedious. But to cycle just for fresh air and exercise, well, that was different. I think she quite enjoyed it.

We used our bicycles for something else, to go from one "pavilion" to another in a local cultural celebration called Caravan. This was quite an imaginative festival. Not far from where we lived in Galley Avenue, in an Orthodox Church, the Greek community put on their show. There were displays of art and costume. There was singing and sometimes even short plays were staged. There was ethnic food. And it was the food that usually was the big draw. Maggie and I cycled some quite long distances to attend three or even four Caravan pavilions in a single evening. There was the Anzac pavilion hosted by Australians and New Zealanders; an Austrian pavilion at the Club Edelweiss, which, sadly, I believe no longer exists; and pavilions celebrating Filipino, Finnish, Italian, Ukrainian, Polish, Hungarian, Spanish, and other cultures. One year, the French and the English got together and did a fantastic joint pavilion. And there was a Newfoundland pavilion that included cod tongues, fish and brewis, and a pair of old codgers who really knew how to handle their fiddle and squeezebox. We took part in Caravan for several years.

Maggie and I had also bought a cottage. It was very minimalist, a drafty four-room box, if one counted the veranda and the loo, and was located in the village of Hastings on the Trent River. It was good to have while we lived in rented accommodation, and we used it for two or three summers, leaving Toronto to drive to Hastings about midnight on Friday and coming back early on Monday morning. We didn't do much there except cut the grass, cook meals on a hibachi, doze in the sun, and read. But it was our little getaway, and I know that Maggie always looked forward to those weekends.

In the summer of 1977, I spent some time in France. Maggie was very involved with her work at the management consulting firm, was enjoying every minute of it, and insisted that I go alone. The purpose was to study French. I did, and it made a considerable difference to my French. And there were other unexpected spinoffs. One of the people I met in the French class was a doctor from Campbellford, which is located, as it happens, just a few miles east of Hastings. David and I hit it off immediately, we got together regularly when we were both back in Canada, and for some time he was Maggie's GP.

David had immigrated to Canada from England in the early 1950s, and he had been associated with the RAF toward the end of World War II. Because of that status, he was always invited to an annual reunion at the military institute in Toronto, and he went often. On one occasion, he invited one of the doctors at his Campbellford clinic to come along. They both turned up. David recalled that, at the door, everyone was invited to sign in and to indicate which service they had been part of. David's colleague, Gus Hoffmann, signed his name and under "Service", he wrote "yes". David asked Gus about this afterward.

"Well", Gus said. "I wasn't going to write 'Luftwaffe'!"

I have left a lot out of this period in Canada. To some extent, it was a time for Maggie and me to find our way, but Maggie seemed to be doing a much better job of it than I. There was a lot of just plain slog, work-related travel for each of us, a fair bit of time out of Toronto and away from each other, but somehow that seemed an acceptable price to pay. Maggie's work was quite different from mine in various ways. Maggie was breaking new ground for herself in many of her management consulting projects, while I seemed to be solving the same problems over and over. Maggie's colleagues were dynamic, interesting, and often a pleasure to be with, whereas I spent little time socializing with my colleagues and found most of my excitement with Maggie and with friends outside work. My impression, quite often, seemed to be that Maggie was forging ahead and that many future possibilities beckoned, whereas I was mostly just treading water.

I didn't speak to Maggie about this, and probably I should have.

Maggie and I had travelled to Canada at my request. She had agreed with no argument. But beginning about ten to fifteen years later and extending right to the present, I have doubted the wisdom in making that request.

But another change in our life was coming, although we were unaware of it until it was right in front of us.

CHAPTER 9

CITY OF DREAMS

Maggie's path through her working life was simply astonishing, and I have tried through this account to present in some detail a picture of the career of my remarkable partner. An important segment of that path, important for both of us, was our move to Vienna. That change came about unexpectedly, as did other aspects of our working lives.

At that point in her career, Maggie had an interesting and exciting job, and she was reluctant to change course. The big element that entered the mix was the need to look closely at an opportunity and decide whether it should be accepted or ignored. That phase of Maggie's career came to an end through that particular opportunity, and once again it was something that could be pinned on me. Or perhaps I should say that Maggie deferred to something that presented itself to me but something that ultimately became ours to share.

At the time, my work was fairly interesting, but there was really nowhere to go. Not that I was a supercharged testosterone addict headed for the top, but I did want more. One day I saw something I wasn't intended to see. It was an advertisement for the job of editor of the *Bulletin* at the International Atomic Energy Agency (IAEA) in Vienna. I showed it to Maggie. I could tell that she really didn't want to leave the consulting firm, but she objected when I proposed just to forget about it. She was adamant that I apply. The chance of me being accepted was probably minimal anyway, she said. "But if they want to interview you, go ahead. Do an interview."

So I applied, then promptly forgot about the whole thing. A little more than a week later, I received a phone call from the UN in New York. Would I be prepared to do a telephone interview? I said yes, and a day and time was agreed on. Maggie and I talked it all over again that evening. The day of the interview came, I spoke to someone from UN Personnel on a call that lasted about twenty minutes, and he concluded by saying that someone would contact me.

Less than a week later, I received a letter. A job offer. At that time, I was thirty-one and Maggie was twenty-eight.

The business of applying for jobs and attending interviews is exciting, a great ego boost. And it can be something that seems to have only an up-side. But when faced by a job offer, things suddenly look different. The meaning of a statement often made by one of my uncles became clear: When you open one door, you close all the others.

Maggie and I talked briefly about the possibility of me being in Vienna and her remaining in Toronto, but neither of us wanted that. The big changes resulting from me accepting the job would be Maggie leaving the consulting firm and me leaving my job at AECL. We would have to break with friends. We had three cats. What would we do with them? And going to Vienna would mean what? Apart from a two-paragraph job description, I had no very clear idea what kind of work I would be doing. We knew nobody in Vienna or even in Austria. We each spoke a little German but not enough, we were convinced, to get along in a German-speaking country. And what would Maggie do? I had sent an inquiry to New York asking about work for spouses. The answer I received said that a spouse could not apply for a job in the UN after moving to Vienna if the job was in the same UN agency where the partner was working. Working in other UN agencies in Vienna was fine, and I soon found that there were several such agencies. But to a great extent, we would be dropping into a dark pit where the possibilities were unknown.

We discussed it intensely for several days. We had almost reached the conclusion that I would write back to the UN and decline the offer. With some reluctance, we were both gravitating to a condition of "no change".

Then I asked Maggie: "If I say no, will we be sitting around twenty years from now wondering what it would be like had we gone to Vienna?"

Maggie thought about that for more than a minute. "You're right", she said. "We're going."

That was late in June 1978. I signed up for an intense week of one-on-one German instruction at the Goethe-Institut, something that was entirely exhausting but later repaid its weight in gold. The UN in Vienna wanted me there at a desk as soon as possible. We lived then in rented furnished accommodation in Toronto and owned very little, so physical encumbrances were few. We had decided to take our cats and found that apart from some quite stringent requirements on their vaccinations and travel documents, the arrangements to do that were straightforward. The UN gave large allowances for moving household effects, but we determined that everything that made sense to take would fit into one large aluminum trunk. Household items were shipped by sea back then, so the time between shipping something at this end and picking it up in Vienna was about five weeks. Cutting this story short, I left first and arrived in Vienna in early August. Maggie shipped the cats by an Air Canada service that was then called Sky Kennel, and Maggie herself arrived in September.

In summary, we decided not to ignore the opportunity. At the time, it looked very one-sided. It was an opportunity for me, but it appeared to be a setback for Maggie. We had concluded that it was an opportunity that would knock only once. And it turned out to be an opportunity the fruits of which we both would share. But back then, it was Maggie who made the toughest decision, and it wasn't the first, or the last, time that she demonstrated just how much she was prepared to invest in us, and that she had the sheer guts to follow what looked like a speculative promise while letting go what seemed to be a large personal advantage. Looking back on that episode, my great good fortune in going through life with Maggie was confirmed in spades.

My first day of work at the IAEA presented mixed surprises. It took little time to realize that my boss could be an awkward and unpleasant man but someone who could be managed provided one took an early decision to stand up to him. I discovered also that my co-workers were a collection of lovely people: two Austrians, one Swiss, one German, and four ex-pat English women who were married to Austrians and permanent residents of Austria. I learned also that my workload would be light and that it was okay to cast about through the agency to find areas where someone having my background could help — find some variety, the added advantage being that I could stay clear of my boss for part of the time. This led me to a Canadian division director, a German project manager, a Swedish wordsmith, an American lawyer, a Finnish fixer, and the most extraordinary collection of Austrians in the print shop. I relayed all this to Maggie by letter (it was pre-email — even the most primitive email — by more than a decade and a half), and she told me about the large amount of work she was having to do to wrap up everything and join me. I felt guilty immediately and said so, but Maggie brushed all that aside saying that, once we were together in Vienna, we could find a new routine. This was not the first time — and definitely not the last — that Maggie's resilience was evident.

My German colleague, Hans, invited me to his home for dinner one evening almost immediately after I started work, and I didn't realize until later how unusual it was for continental Europeans to do this. The standard practice was that one could meet one's colleagues in a pub or restaurant but not in their home. Home was for close family, and exceptions to this close-family rule were very rare. But Hans had experience in non-European settings, and he guessed that I might be adrift and friendless in Vienna. I got to know Hans and his wife, Ursula, quite well, and Ursula and I remain in contact today.

Another colleague, Dilys, had a friend who had lived in Kenya for more than twenty years but who owned an apartment in Vienna that was vacant and that she was willing to rent. The rent requested was very reasonable, and I accepted immediately. Finding a place to live, something I thought might take weeks, had been accomplished in days. Fortunately, the flat was furnished. The apartment was in Vienna's thirteenth district, in an area known as Hietzing. It was an attractive area, and the apartment building was a low-rise four-storey that contained about a dozen apartments. It was on a street called Elsslergasse, named after Fanny Elssler, a nineteenth-century

Viennese ballet dancer. Large walnut trees lined the street on both sides, and each autumn there were walnuts for the taking, many more falling from the trees than all the people living on the street were willing or able to collect.

A third colleague, Gabi, dealt entirely with press clippings. Gabi had worked for the *New York Times* for a decade or so, and her English was good. But she encouraged me to speak German at every opportunity, and although she was more than twenty years older than me, she became a good friend.

Once Maggie arrived in Vienna, she set about looking for work immediately. She applied to OPEC and had a searing experience of misogyny there. She put out feelers at the agency where I worked, and to her surprise she was offered a low-level job in the IAEA library, which she took without hesitation. We wondered about the spouse rule but carefully didn't comment. Not surprisingly, Maggie made her presence felt immediately. She was recognized as someone who, in just a few days, had got to know her way around the library, was willing to work, could work fast without making mistakes, and always had a smile. In no time, she was busy and in demand. We both got to know many people throughout the agency, me because I was in the Public Information department, and Maggie because she became a known feature in the library, where traffic was high.

At that time and perhaps still today, quite a few people took a position at the UN to round off the last few years of their careers. To a considerable extent, we were the odd ones out. Maggie and I found that there was a group of about thirty people in the IAEA who, like us, were in their late twenties and early thirties. We got to know most of those people. We got to know all the Canadians, and when the suggestion was raised to have a "Canadian lunch" once a month, Maggie and I jumped in. Our monthly Canadian lunches soon attracted twenty-five to thirty people. Other nationalities tried the same thing, but only one of them made it work: the Icelanders. Since there were only two people in the IAEA from Iceland, we felt that didn't count.

An opportunity came up for Maggie to move to the United Nations Industrial Development Organization (UNIDO). She accepted it but quickly found it didn't live up to its billing. There was no time to mope, however, because once again, Maggie was headhunted. This time it was by a small UN agency that had been told that, because of shortage of space in New York and abundance of space in Vienna, it was moving from New York to Vienna, regardless of how the staff felt about that. This was the United Nations Commission on International Trade Law (UNCITRAL). The head of that commission was a shrewd cookie, and he screwed out of the UN everything he could to compensate for the inconvenience and unpopularity of the New York to Vienna move. They were to have a new library. Their existing stock of books and directories was to be upgraded. And he wanted somebody with a track record on information and libraries to head that effort — not to be saddled by some time-serving desk jockey dug out of an obscure UN backroom. He wanted to make the choice himself. And he did choose.

Guess who?

Somehow he found Maggie, made her an offer she would never have refused, and she went to work with a will. Setting up a new library and getting it running smoothly was a perfect job for her and she loved it.

My colleagues soon learned about Maggie and were eager to meet her. So when she arrived in Vienna, there was a flurry of introductions as Maggie was welcomed. Maggie was a hit with every one of my work colleagues, and she made friends quickly in the various UN libraries where she worked during our time in Vienna: in the IAEA library, the library of UNIDO, and the library of UNCITRAL.

When I started work in Vienna, the IAEA was located centrally, in a stately old building on the Kärntnerring not far from Schwartzenbergplatz. Maggie and I both worked in that building for a time, Maggie moving soon to a different building when she took a position with UNIDO. In early summer of 1979, all the UN agencies in Vienna were moved to a new United Nations complex (called UNO City), which was located east of the Danube on Wagramerstrasse. Maggie moved there as well, since that coincided with her being headhunted to establish and take over operation of the new library for UNCITRAL. Maggie and I spent the rest of our time in Vienna working in that new complex.

Our new offices were a change from the old building in central Vienna. They were modern. The design of the complex was dramatic and consisted of about a half-dozen semi-circular towers of different heights surrounding a central circular pod and connected at various levels by walkways. Although the building design was arresting, the curved walls offered a challenge for some of the office fittings. Unless they were curved, bookcases and shelving required some imaginative fittings to fix them to the walls. In setting up the UNCITRAL library, Maggie responded to this challenge in her usual imaginative way. Despite members of the UN maintenance staff declaring that what she was proposing was impossible (*"unmöglich"*), she dug in and insisted, and soon the impossible became the acceptable. We had both learned that *"unmöglich"* not only meant "impossible"; it could also mean "I don't want to do that", "It will cost too much", "We've never done it that way before", "It will need approval", and any of a number of other delaying tactics.

There was one aspect of the new buildings that Maggie didn't like at all. Many pieces of art were commissioned to be hung in the new complex, and most of these pieces were very large since in the common areas excluding hallways, there were huge expanses of wall space available. Vienna has always been known for avant-garde art, and many of the large pieces were reminiscent of the work of artists like Egon Schiele, Oskar Kokoschka, Gustav Klimt, and others — except that the commissioned art in the UN complex invited less favourable commentary. Maggie's commentary was not at all favourable, and she would avoid certain areas so that she didn't have to face images that she described as body parts brutally torn from their owners. If pressed she would identify the body parts, and they were mostly tongues and penises.

However, there were many good things about the new complex. Vienna is a very musical city, and it was quite common to have young music students come into the building and provide impromptu concerts in the hallways on the violin, flute, clarinet, or other instruments. People would come out of their offices and listen for ten or fifteen minutes. The cafeteria in the building was large and served excellent meals at low prices. There was also a long outdoor balcony associated with the cafeteria where one could sit in the sun and finish lunch with coffee or a glass of wine. The UN had a commissary where one could buy a range of wines, beers, spirits, and packaged-food items, all tax free and made even more economical at the cash desk on presentation of special "coupons". Friday afternoons saw something of a run on the commissary, since groups of UN staff would relax in their offices and slide into the weekend, lubricated by a couple of bottles of sekt.

There was a distinction between staff hired internationally, such as Maggie and me, and staff hired locally, mostly to admin positions. Staff hired internationally were issued a monthly allowance of coupons for alcohol and tobacco. Those commissary coupons gave rise to a sort of "black market" for services, and Maggie and I made good use of that. Neither of us smoked, and our allocation of alcohol coupons far exceeded our needs. Coupons we didn't use could be passed under the table to maintenance staff or people in the print shop in exchange for favours, such as special service or service at very short turnaround times. It was formally forbidden to do this, but I knew of no instance when that rule was enforced, and a carton or two of cigarettes or a case of good wine was often enough to make a project manager look like a hero.

The building also had its odd side. The mail delivery system through the building relied on plastic bins being carried from the sorting room in the basement to the offices on a system of elevators and conveyor belts installed in the walls and in spaces between floors. It looked good in principle, but it was the case from time to time that a bin would become derailed, there would be a pile-up, and part of the system would need to be shut down while somebody crawled to the scene of the problem and set things right.

A similar system led to more immediate consequences in the cafeteria. People who had finished lunch deposited trays of plates, glasses, cutlery and so forth on shelves at one spot in the cafeteria. An elevator and conveyor system then carried these trays and their contents to the kitchen through a space in the ceiling above the dining area. You can probably guess what happened.

Maggie and I were having lunch with some colleagues one day when we heard shrieks from elsewhere in the dining area. People were jumping up from their seats to avoid a hail of rice, peas, chicken bones, and other detritus that was tumbling down on them and their plates through slats in the ceiling. Despite all that, the UN buildings in Vienna were a good place to work.

During our time in Vienna, both of us honed our political instincts, but this was particularly true for Maggie. Everything in the UN had the potential to become some sort of political game. The head of UNCITRAL (and the man who had selected Maggie), a tall Dutchman named Willem, had a stern expression that tended to cow everyone, something that irritated him. Maggie's first approach was always to deal with someone on an open and person-to-person basis. If someone showed themselves to be pompous or arrogant or just a twit, then she could modify the approach as needed. But most of the time her initial approach paid off. Willem was a good fifteen inches taller than Maggie, but rather than being cowed, she would smile at him and say something like, "Just tell me what you want, Willem. Out with it."

As Maggie found with other powerful managers later, the direct approach, avoiding any bowing and scraping, was something they appreciated.

One of our early surprises in Vienna was how quickly we were accepted by some of the people in the UN, people with whom we had no common background. That's how we found out about Küniglberg. Küniglberg is a hill that rises to a height of 250 metres in Hietzing, the district of Vienna where we lived. That hill had significance for Maggie and me because of two things: It lay between where Maggie and I lived and where my colleague Gabi Aichinger lived; and at the top of Küniglberg were offices and studios of the Austrian Broadcasting Service, the ORF Zentrum, where the Österreichische Rundfunk was located.

Gabi lived on her own, about a fifteen-minute walk from our apartment in Elsslergasse. Gabi's place was a very large single house, and the entire ground floor was usually rented to someone, while Gabi lived on the spacious upper floor. Gabi practically adopted me from the moment I began working in the Public Information office, and, within a few days of my starting date I was invited to her place. Gabi also insisted on meeting Maggie as soon as she arrived, and this happened as soon as Maggie had overcome her travel fatigue.

Maggie and Gabi got along almost like daughter and mother, and we were both invited regularly for a glass of wine or four and a chat; to watch a television programme with her; for a meal; and most frequently, for all the above. We went often on Sunday afternoon, when three or four ladies Gabi's age were invited for coffee and cakes, *Kaffee und Kuchen*. On those occasions, the conversation was all in German, and Maggie and I contributed where and when we could. But those contributions became more frequent and more competent after only a few months in Vienna.

Maggie and I listened to the news in German on television every day. Since the news was repeated each hour, we had second and third chances to figure out what was being said, so the news became an important element in our German instruction.

Gabi's ladies also listened to the news, particularly the news at 9:00 p.m. The news reader at that hour was always the same, and he had a resonant, mellifluous, and utterly masculine baritone that, by their own admission, set off all Gabi's ladies. This was so much the case that two of them who lived close to the ORF studios would look out at about nine thirty, hoping to catch a glimpse of the news reader as he walked home.

Gabi's favourite meal, and one that she prepared most often for Maggie and me, was roast chicken with sauerkraut and a mixed salad generously dressed with garlic flavoured oil. The roast chicken came out of Gabi's oven brown, crispy, sprinkled in herbs, and delicious. The sauerkraut, prepared using small amounts of apple and bacon pieces, was stewed for hours. The whole meal was washed down by what seemed to be Gabi's inexhaustible supply of rosé from Burgenland. The garlic in Gabi's salad ensured that any artery-clogging potential of fats from the chicken was neutralized instantly. Indeed, having returned home from Gabi's lovely dinners, we found that it was common for us to awaken at 2:00 a.m. overheated, having a pulse rate above ninety, and our skin seeming to be covered everywhere by a film of garlic oil.

The walk to and from Gabi's place was pleasant. From Elsslergasse we crossed a main road, Lainzerstrasse, to a pedestrian path called Alois Kraus Allee, and this took us to a delightful, steep cobbled lane called Puttlingen Gasse. Puttlingen Gasse rose up the side of Küniglberg and emptied into Pacassistrasse. From there, we climbed farther to Konrad Duden Gasse, which then branched into Geneegasse, where Gabi lived.

One evening while returning home from Gabi's place, we came across a baby hedgehog. For Maggie, hedgehogs were a symbol of everything that is enchanting and vulnerable in our world. She picked up that little hedgehog and talked to it before depositing it back in the grass. That is one of the many precious images I have of Maggie.

Not far from Gabi's home was a superb restaurant nestled among houses and surrounded by hazelnut hedges. That restaurant was called the Biedermeyer Stube and was a classic place. Everything on the menu came in generous portions, and Gabi and her local friends would gather there regularly. There was a large flagstone patio and, in season, it was always full for Saturday and Sunday lunches. The place was owned and run by two large jovial brothers. They were inveterate jokers. They would repeat people's orders, mangling the names effortlessly, as when one of them wrote down Maggie's order on one occasion, repeating it as Piprikaschnatzel (instead of Parikaschnitzel). On another occasion he caught Maggie looking at his large stomach and said to her privately, "*Das ist mein Backhendlfriedhof.*" (That's my roast chicken cemetery.) Maggie and I were flattered always to be invited to join Gabi's Viennese crowd there, and although, even after two years, we failed to understand everything that was said, it was clear that we were always more than welcome. I watched the way the ladies looked at Maggie. Her smile was able to charm people even across a language barrier.

There were so many aspects of Vienna and surrounding areas that we explored. It would be tedious for me to relate them all. So I will write about only three.

Schönbrunn

The apartment Maggie and I had was about a ten-minute walk from Schönbrunn Palace. The palace itself was lovely, but we spent almost all our time there in the garden, which is massive. It contains immaculately trimmed hedges that stretch for several hundred metres behind the palace itself, as well as shady walks, statuary, colourful flower beds, and plenty of places to sit and ponder. Maggie and I went there many times, usually on weekends, and often taking a picnic lunch.

Rust

As one drives out of Vienna across the Danube to the east, one enters a very large flat plain, and that portion of it in Lower Austria is dotted with oil pumps because this is Austria's oil producing district. Production isn't massive, but it is carefully looked after.

Going farther east, one heads toward the Neusiedler See, a large shallow lake that is partly in Austria and partly in Hungary. When Maggie and I were in Vienna (1978–1980) the Soviet Union was still in full cry, and there was a string of goon towers across the Neusiedler See. Of course, those towers were intended to keep Hungarians in

Hungary, not as the propaganda had it, to keep Austrians from fleeing to the workers' paradise.

On the Austrian side of the lake, there is a village called Rust. It is called that because most of the chimneys are capped by storks' nests (roosts). It is a lovely spot, and we would pass an entire day there, walking the streets, having a nice lunch, and admiring the well-kept houses and gardens. A well-known painter, Gottfried Kumpf, produced a painting of Rust, and Maggie and I paid what we thought was then a princely sum for a print of that painting. I am looking at it as I write this, and I can picture our visits there as clearly as if they occurred yesterday.

KREMS AND DÜRNSTEIN

Driving upstream from Vienna along the Danube, one passes the great hill called Kahlenberg, which is part of the last of the Alpine foothills. About thirty kilometres or so farther on, one comes to the town of Krems, nestled in an area known as the Weinviertel, and indeed there are some superb wines produced in this area. Krems is also known for its mustard, and apart from riesling there is a classic wine from this area, one that Maggie and I bought a lot of and enjoyed greatly. That wine is grüner veltliner.

Not far from Krems is Dürnstein, known for its hilltop castle, which was where Richard the Lionheart was incarcerated after he was abducted on his way back home from a crusade in the Holy Land and held for ransom. One can walk up to the castle, but Maggie and I always preferred to sit by the river and enjoy a sausage and some wine. Below Dürnstein Castle and close to the river is the Hotel Restaurant Sanger Blondel. Blondel has gone into legend in what must be a most romantic way. A French poet, it seems, Blondel somehow became associated with Richard the Lionheart and went searching for him. Blondel apparently caught sight of someone he thought was Richard through a window in Dürnstein Castle. Blondel was a minstrel, and he sang verses that both he and Richard knew, managing to confirm somehow that the man he saw really was Richard. Blondel is credited in part with Richard's escape from Dürnstein Castle, either through Blondel's direct help or by alerting others who then sprang the king.

Krems was a favourite spot for Maggie and me. We must have gone there more than a dozen times during our stay in Vienna, always in summer. I think that Maggie felt some kind of English connection with Dürnstein Castle, even though she would readily admit that Richard was not a great king.

Our two-year stay in Vienna eventually came to an end. I was offered a further two years, but the offer was so ham-fisted I turned it down. Besides, staying away from one's home base too long could leave one stranded, something that had happened to other Canadians in Vienna. Maggie left in June 1980 to go back to Toronto via England, and I left in early August. Once she was back and established in Toronto, I could send the cats home.

Maggie was my lovely damsel in Vienna, young, full of life, and rejoicing in the ability to make friends with people from all around the world. The first few months in Vienna were tense until we learned the ropes and realized that we had not torpedoed our futures irretrievably.

In Vienna we lived, loved, ate, drank, and saw the world in microcosm. In Vienna we learned and grew. From Vienna we travelled over a fair part of Southern Europe. And I like to think that we left Vienna as different and more mature people.

CHAPTER 10

RESETTLED BUT...

It was from Galley Avenue that Maggie and I moved to Vienna. When I look back on it, I see that move, a return to Europe, as a significant break. The two years we spent in Vienna were a defining hiatus. At the end of those two years, when we returned to Toronto, our life together seemed to move off in a different direction. Perhaps because our time in Vienna had been a considerable confidence boost. Perhaps because the experience we had gained from the Vienna detour demonstrated clearly enough that we were much more established as successful working professionals. Perhaps because we were now members of the first IKEA generation, were leaving behind the lives of struggling young ex-students, had jettisoned our bricks-and-planks bookcases. Perhaps because we could see some real future prospects. Or perhaps just because we had acquired some steel, tempered by our time in a different part of our world.

After Vienna, we entered into a long period of varied successes for both of us. Maggie, in particular, carved a path that was uniquely varied and delivered great satisfaction. Looking back, I find that it was one great fantastic voyage. As I write this in May of 2022, my life with Maggie in now behind me. To produce this book, I needed to delve into some far corners of my memory, and I have been surprised at the amount of detail that has welled up. While struggling to deal with a huge loss, I have recalled enormous amounts of "good stuff"; in some cases that has been very much a bittersweet experience, but in many cases I have smiled and even laughed at some tender and joyous memories.

I have also tried to look back closely at different periods of Maggie's and my life together, wanting to recover my impressions from back then. From 1980 onward, Maggie and I had moved into that period one might refer to as confident young adults, pushing forward into life. Maggie was happy and I can sense even now the depth and strength of her happiness at our life together. From our base in Toronto, we travelled a good deal and we enjoyed it very much. We had accumulated, even then, a wealth of life experiences that were beyond what I could have expected. I think that Maggie's view of the world had changed somewhat, but my view of the world was altered fundamentally. I believe that I had approached Maggie's basic European outlook more closely. I think this was a product of three things: the realization of how my rather flat and restricted North American view of the world had become more richly European as a result of the time I had spent with Maggie in England; because of our having risen to meet the social, linguistic, and occupational challenges posed during our two years in Vienna; and simply our coming closer together and functioning as a couple who now had some miles and experience under our belts. But I realized eventually that this also posed a problem.

The problem can be stated in blunt, if perhaps exaggerated terms: If I felt more European, what was I doing in Canada?

I struggled with the feeling that our decision, or perhaps more accurately, my request that we come to Canada in 1974, was not for the best. Thinking back from today and trying to recall what yesterday was like involves, almost certainly, a distortion, since I am seeing things through the sad mist of having lost Maggie. I'm quite sure that I suffered survivor guilt in the months following Maggie's death, and that I'm still struggling with it. I'm convinced that that feeling isn't going away any time soon.

So did I do the right thing all those years ago? Would Maggie have been happier had we made our life in England? I won't ever know the answer to that or even whether it's a sensible question.

When Maggie returned to Canada in June, instead of coming directly to Toronto she flew on to Edmonton to visit some friends. Not all the arrangements worked out as planned, however. Maggie's bags weren't transferred to the Edmonton flight and languished instead somewhere in Pearson Airport in Toronto. Maggie made a call from Edmonton to a friend in Toronto who schlepped out to the airport, found the bags, managed to have them released to him, and called Maggie back to say that everything was fine. The odd aspect of this was that Maggie had worn her dirndl on the flight from London. But a dirndl can be a little tight around the top, you see, and it was some time before Maggie was able to go to a shop in Edmonton and buy something more practical. I'm not sure that Maggie ever wore the dirndl again.

Back in Toronto, Maggie found a house to rent in Etobicoke, and it took very little searching for her to find a spot at another large management consulting firm. By the time I returned to Toronto in early August of 1980, we had living quarters, the cats were back home, and Maggie was well into her new job. That job basically began where her previous management consulting job left off, but this time she was a fully functioning management consultant. As in her earlier consulting work, she rose easily to the challenges that came along. Maggie's new projects led her into areas where she had little previous experience but she mastered all these new areas quickly. Once again, there were some late nights. There were after-work blowouts. There was some entertaining. And Maggie was making contacts that would serve her well.

When I had left to go to Vienna, my supervisor, who was one of the most extraordinary men I have known, gave me an enormous pay increase, which took effect the day after I left, and he also made my departure a secondment. This meant that his budget took no hit, and that I had a guaranteed job to return to. The kicker was that no specific job was defined. On my return, I found something within AECL and worked at it for a few weeks, until an opportunity arose for me to move into the full technical stream. I grasped that with both hands. The sort of technical work I began then defined the direction my work would take over the rest of my career.

So life settled down again in Toronto, and Maggie and I both dug into our work. We were moving into a new phase, but what this meant would not become obvious immediately.

We both met interesting new people, and several of those people formed part of our lives from then on. The house Maggie had rented was owned by a young Italian chap, a recent immigrant, who I think had visions of a quick fortune. It wasn't at all that he was grasping; it just seemed that he expected life in the land of plenty to pour a generous flow of coin into his coffers. The house had quite a few problems, but we expected not to stay a long time. It sat on a double lot, and behind it was a large vegetable garden. Our landlord had carpetted that garden space in a forest of tomato plants, apparently visualizing gallons of pasta sauce. And gallons of the stuff eventually did materialize. But unfortunately, he also planted a number of zucchini plants. These things stretched across the entire garden like triffids, and Maggie decided one day to go out and hack away the jungle of tendrils. Maggie knew, but apparently our landlord didn't, that zucchini are very cagey. You go out to inspect, find four or five delicate little zucchini almost ready to harvest, and decide to do that the next day. The next day, however, they have transformed themselves into giant two-foot-long marrows, not of much use for anything. Maggie decided to harvest a basketful of zucchini that were still zucchini. In the process, she heard a faint gnawing sound.

I learned of this discovery when Maggie came into the house in something of a flap and told me there was a horrible monster in the garden. And there was. It was a tomato worm, a lime green, bulbous, four-inch-long Michelin man insect sporting a nasty looking black spike on its mouth end. Maggie had never seen a tomato worm, never heard of one, and was openly sceptical. But she agreed to look it up the next day at work while I quietly crushed the little sod.

We lived and worked through the rest of that summer and autumn, into the winter, and then into the following year. With little effort, we had slid back into life in Toronto. But as the months passed, our social calendar became full, partly because of getting together with long-standing friends and partly because of Maggie's new friends at work. My new friends at work were almost all engineers. There were limitations there. Having an engineer wax enthusiastic about his new slide rule at a party is something that has limited social appeal. So for some months, Maggie made her daily trek to Bay and King, and I struggled along the QEW to Sheridan Park. But things were set for another series of big changes.

After our return to Toronto from Vienna, Maggie had deposited resumes with her various professional associations, since anyone looking for people to staff a library would be likely to check those associations for prospective candidates. And then we had both forgotten about those resumes. Maggie had been in her post-Vienna job at the consulting firm about two years. She came home from work one day saying that her resume at a library association had been found by a company, and they had made an initial approach to her. Maggie said that an interview had been set up three days hence. To have this fall out of the sky, on top of the ongoing excitement that working at the consulting firm delivered, left Maggie reeling somewhat. But I could tell from the sparkle in her eyes that she wouldn't have it any other way. Maggie hesitated, only slightly, over just one thing: the company she would be interviewing was a large chemical company and Maggie wondered why she would be of interest to them.

"I know nothing about chemicals or chemical companies", she said.

"Perhaps not", I agreed. "But you know a lot about libraries and business. And", I added, "not everyone can point to the UN as a past employer. I suspect that a company looking at that and probably not knowing much about the UN might well be impressed."

For once in my life, I had pegged something exactly right. Maggie attended the interview, and one of the areas the interviewer focussed on was Maggie's UN experience. Maggie laid it all out for the interviewer: how the IAEA library was set up; its online system, which was cutting edge at the time; and the fact that it had to service so many different groups of users. The interviewer was just as interested in the UNCITRAL library. The fact that Maggie had set up that library from nothing and then ran it prompted many questions. It was only a few weeks later that Maggie was asked back for a second interview, and when it was clear that she was interested, the company tabled a job offer on the spot.

Maggie brought the offer home in a state of high excitement. We both looked it over, it looked excellent, and Maggie contacted the company the next day and accepted.

This was only one of a number of quite major changes that took place about then. Maggie's new place of work would be at Yonge and Sheppard, and the experience of going to her interviews demonstrated clearly enough that the trek from Etobicoke to North York, involving three changes on public transit, was just too time consuming. We had been considering buying a house, and so we began right away looking seriously at possibilities.

Things moved forward at a brisk pace. Maggie began work at the chemical company. There was a hornet's nest of company politics to deal with. The library there was a high-cost overhead item that had been passed around from department to department, each department being eager to dump it somewhere else once they realized the cost they had to shoulder.

That job was a defining one for Maggie. By that time, she had had enough experience in the business world to know how to read a balance sheet and to know what the options were for any organization that wanted to cut costs. One prominent view within the company was that the library should be closed and that the information needed should bought externally. Maggie's faith in the value, both intrinsic and financial, of libraries would not let her believe that that option made any sense whatever. Looking through all the possibilities, she concluded that identifying the details of the library users and the nature and extent of their use of the library would make it clear whether she could sell the idea of charging back library costs to its users and whether she could make it work in practice.

Once Maggie had the basic data and had digested it, she was almost ecstatic. What the data told her was that a charge-back approach could work. She floated the idea past her boss who found it interesting but who was VERY sceptical. Maggie asked him if he had any objection to her approaching his boss, a very senior man in the company. Her boss said okay, but with one proviso: "Don't get me into trouble."

The man in charge, John, was something like Willem at UNCITRAL, and Maggie decided to use exactly the same approach she had used with Willem. John was a large man, tall and solidly built, and he displayed what seemed to be a slight perennial scowl. I would have loved to attend that first meeting Maggie had with him. But I suspect that Maggie's brilliant smile, her direct approach, her fearless but friendly manner in dealing with someone who outranked her seriously, and her ability to present an argument in a concise and convincing way, these probably carried the day. The man in charge wanted a plan. Maggie set to work.

I will shorten this story now. Maggie convinced John, and they became as close to being colleagues as their separation along the chain of corporate command would allow. Maggie invested enormous amounts of personal effort to understand who her library clients were, what they needed, what they were being supplied, and of what value to them were those products and services. She talked to her customers every chance she got and on every level — professional, technical, social. Slowly, she sold the idea of a charge-back library across the company. I think that her sheer human appeal had a lot to do with this. The new persona of the library took shape, and the different groups of customers recognized their interest in making this new format of library work and in working with Maggie to define and receive the kinds of library service they wanted and needed.

Maggie enjoyed her time at the chemical company immensely. This was partly because she had taken on a truly large challenge and produced something new and exciting in response. It was also partly because she learned so much in her nine years there. Maggie wrote perhaps a dozen conference papers based on that experience, including knowing a library's customers and their needs, knowing how a library delivers value to its users and how to quantify that value, seeing a library as a business and understanding how to operate that business and track its performance financially, and quite a few other items that stunned me at the time in their clarity and originality but whose details are now lost. At the chemical company, Maggie learned a great deal about business and she would apply that knowledge in all her future jobs. There came a point when Maggie was convinced that she had done all she could at the chemical company and that it was time to move on. She began looking. It seemed natural to try to parley her nine years' experience in the chemical industry, but all Maggie's efforts along those lines led to disappointing dead ends. Among other chemical companies, there seemed to be little interest in what she was able to do, and the few things they did offer, she wasn't prepared to consider. Once again, the way forward revealed itself unexpectedly.

Word had got round in the library world about Maggie's success in the chemical company library, and she received a feeler from an unexpected quarter. The Toronto Public Library was looking at the possibility of a fee-for-service research function, to be made available in person or online through the Reference Library at 789 Yonge Street. There were discussions. Maggie was vaguely interested but knew that there would be problems and that few of them would be technical. But she agreed to take on the project provided it had a two-year time limit. Whether or not the service was up and running by then, Maggie would leave after two years. I have often wondered what would have happened had the two years elapsed but the service still was not functioning. I doubt that Maggie would have just walked away from a situation like that. She wasn't one to quit easily, and when she became determined to make something happen, anyone who stood in the way was in for a rough ride.

Maggie started work. One of the first tasks was to find a name for this new service, and they eventually settled on IntelliSearch. Measures were taken early to make people aware that this service was being put in place and how it would work. Advertising of various low-key forms was mounted. The bush telegraph went into action. A few months in, a legal letter arrived on Maggie's desk. It was from somewhere in the United States, and it was a demand to cease and desist using the name IntelliSearch because it was a name protected in some American jurisdiction. Maggie consulted the legal department and asked them to write back telling the lawyer basically to shove it. In the end, something like that happened. The American complainant had somehow forgotten (or wasn't even aware) that American law didn't extend across an international border. IntelliSearch at the Toronto Public Library remained in place.

In setting up such a fee-for-service function, the basic problem was not a difficult one, and given the size and richness of the reference library's holdings, the approach did make sense. There was the question of finding staff who were savvy enough commercially to be able to approach the work in the right frame of mind. That turned out not to be a holding item. The problem was resistance that came from elsewhere.

The library was unionized and there was a deep dislike for any approach that wanted to charge fees for making use of information that had been assembled at public expense. "Information should be free" was the rallying cry. Maggie had many meetings with the people who stood firm on this idea. She never convinced them that it was a blinkered ideological approach. She agreed fully with the notion that the library's holdings were a public asset. But she made the case that finding what someone wanted in that large store of information always would take time and effort. In that sense, finding the information that someone wanted and putting it in their hands was not a cost-free exercise. And it didn't really matter whether the person doing the searching was an ordinary Jane or Joe, or a skilled or experienced researcher. The point Maggie made was that the mantra "information should be free" was based on a misguided and misleading concept. What probably irritated the "information should be free" crowd most was that they couldn't deny this argument. The project went ahead, with the library management's blessing. The resistance never went away, however, and Maggie simply had to put up with what turned out to be continuous heckling and pushback.

When the service actually started up, clients tried it and most found it to be a good deal. Maggie had two staff, and the business built up quickly. By her two-year deadline, she was able to hand it over to someone else and walk away. IntelliSearch still functions within the Toronto Public Library.

As in the past, Maggie allowed herself some time to reorient and figure out what would come next, but "what would come next" appeared on its own more quickly than she expected. A local business that specialized in electronic databases and was a force in the information industry in Canada became interested in recruiting Maggie almost immediately. By this time in her career, Maggie knew most people in the library-and-information world in Canada, at least by name, and many people knew her. Discussions with this company were successful, and Maggie was taken on to lead the group that offered training and troubleshooting as the Canadian agents for a service based in California. The local company, Micromedia, had a wide range of interests but seemed to struggle somewhat in their dealings with the California service, Dialog. Maggie and her group ultimately became responsible for training and servicing Dialog customers all across Canada. This meant that Maggie and three or four other trainers had to schedule training for groups and organizations across the country and in both French and English. In essence, Maggie was running a business based on Dialog within the larger business Micromedia. Maggie's experience in running the chemical company's library as a business within a business was crucial here. At least one colleague from that time has marvelled at Maggie's creativity, productivity, and ability to pull rabbits out of hats whenever that was necessary.

During this period of Maggie's career, which lasted about eight years, she was out of Toronto about one week per month on average. It was during this time that I learned to cook. We both had busy work lives, but I did accompany Maggie on a number of her trips. We spent a lovely few days in St. John's, a trip that didn't deliver much financial return because of the small population and the small information industry and industrial base in Newfoundland. But Maggie felt it was necessary to show that the people there mattered, that their problems were just as important to them as was the case for people in larger centres. Maggie loved dealing with her customers on the East Coast, and she always found a very warm welcome there. I carried bags for both of us on several occasions when Maggie was obliged to attend the annual meeting in California that brought together the Dialog representatives from countries around the world. Dialog was located in Palo Alto. During Maggie's downtime, this was a good base from which to explore the vineyards of Napa and Sonoma; parts of San Francisco; and areas south of San Francisco — along the coast to delightful small cities like Carmel and to the Monterey aquarium, as well as areas farther inland.

Maggie and her colleagues visited customers in towns and cities across Canada, although the focus was on Toronto, Ottawa, Montreal, and Vancouver because of the concentration of population and industry. But there were visits to smaller cities. One memorable visit was to Whitehorse in February. That year and during the time of our visit there, temperatures in Toronto were low, -20 to -25°C for days on end, whereas Whitehorse was enjoying a relative heat wave. Temperatures in Whitehorse were in the low positive single digits and snow was melting. We were sitting in a restaurant in Whitehorse having lunch one warm day, and the server discovered we were from Toronto.

"Why would you come here from Toronto in February?" she asked.

Maggie's response was immediate.

"To get away from the cold."

During her time at Micromedia, Maggie's Dialog business always turned a profit, and her income numbers were always within a few percentage points of the numbers she predicted. She was considered a star.

Maggie had a good run at Micromedia, but it all unravelled because of machinations at the head office in California. Dialog discontinued Micromedia's role as the representative for Canada. Maggie made sure that her staff all moved to other positions; nobody in her group was made redundant.

Except for Maggie. Maggie knew that she would be able to find something else, but she was less sure about her staff.

Micromedia found a few things for her to do, but eventually she left. In her final acts at Micromedia, looking out for her staff's future, Maggie demonstrated her true nature as a compassionate and caring supervisor and as a good person.

CHAPTER 11

A PLACE OF OUR OWN

Although the following thirty years and more were spent in Canada, by no means was it all just "more of the same". Maggie's life changed, mostly because of the number of jobs and the great variety of work she took on over that period but also partly because both our working lives involved greater variety and somewhat greater complexity. This was partly because our work placed larger and more interesting demands on us both, partly because of new friends, and partly because of events that occurred in Maggie's family.

In November 1982, we let our friends know that we were actively looking to buy a house. They thought we were crazy. Mortgage interest rates were at 17 percent. Entirely the wrong time to be looking at house purchase. But Maggie and I had built up a large nest egg that we had always intended to use as a down payment. The deciding factor, however, turned out to be the upside of stratospheric mortgage interest rates. And that was the fact that almost nobody was buying, so in order for a house to sell, its price had to be favourable. A little bit of looking showed us houses that had been on the market for ages and whose asking prices had been slashed by as much as 75 percent over the space of eight or nine months. So I bought a couple of newspapers, took a day off work, and went around looking at a short list of ten houses for sale that I thought were suitable. To be "suitable", a house had to be on the main north-south Yonge subway line to make Maggie's commute to her work at the chemical company at Yonge and Sheppard reasonably short. It also had to be close enough to central Toronto that my commute to Sheridan Park was tolerable. And we really wanted to be in an older area close to Toronto's cultural centre, close to things that we had begun taking advantage of. We also wanted it to be close to the friends we got together with regularly. I narrowed this list to three houses, then asked our real estate agent to set up visits to them so that Maggie and I could view them together. We homed in quite quickly on one of these houses, which was at 84 Shaftesbury Avenue, just east of Yonge Street at the corner of Ottawa Street, and about five blocks south of Yonge and St. Clair.

The owner wanted to sell. Maggie loved the place. And after a short series of offers one evening, both sides signed off. We now owned a house. At that point, in December of 1982, we thought it would be good for some time, but we had no inkling that we would live there for the next thirty years.

The implications of this move into a house involved two important strands. We wanted to find the best and quickest way to get out from under some serious mortgage interest. And I was leaving regular employment to strike out on my own. In hindsight, I blanch at the freewheeling way we handled these large life changes, but we were young and confident and didn't know any better. In the end, it all worked out. Maggie and I had great jobs, we were doing interesting work, we were bringing in good money, and we soon put our personal marks on 84 Shaftesbury Avenue.

The house had immediate appeal, being a classic Victorian house built in 1874, and our move resulted in aspects of our life being redirected. We soon recognized that we would need to sell the cottage. We just weren't making enough use of it, because so much time needed to be devoted to our new house, including planning some modifications. These modifications weren't the result of discoveries of the "full panic and drop everything" sort. They were necessary repairs to be done at some point, and some things that were nice-to-haves.

The house was long and narrow, barely eighteen feet wide and almost eighty feet long at the ground-floor level. It was three floors, four if one counted the basement. Our bedroom was a spacious, airy, sun-drenched nest, but a big nest, right at the top of the house. The distance from the floor to the highest point in the ceiling under the northward sloping roof of that bedroom was more than twelve feet. On that top level, there was also a bathroom. The next floor down included two small bedrooms, a bathroom, and a large south-facing room that became our den, library, and television room. On the ground floor, there was a long living and dining space at the front of the house and a generous kitchen with breakfast area at the rear. A large sliding-glass door opened out from the kitchen to a back garden space. The basement was partly finished and was used by the previous owners for storage and had a corner reserved for ironing.

Over the years, particularly at the hands of the previous owner, extensions and some major changes had been made. The large airy top bedroom and adjoining bathroom had been one of them. A half basement had been dug under the front portion of the house, and this had included the introduction of reinforced concrete walls that were probably good for a Richter 10 seismic event.

The front of the house had bay windows on both the ground and first floors, and its exterior finish was brick painted grey. The long west outside wall of the house was covered in stucco, and we soon discovered that this needed work. In the back garden was a crab apple tree that put on a brilliant display in spring despite its age, a small honeysuckle bush, and an extravagant mock orange shrub (*philadelphus coronarius*), which produced floods of virginal white blossoms in those years when it wasn't taking a floral sabbatical. We eventually installed a "Wendy house" (another Walker family reference, this time to *Peter Pan*) in the garden against the back fence, where we kept garden tools and my bicycle. The front of the house rose to a steep peak, and the gables were decorated in white-painted wooden jigsaw ornamentation, making our home something that Maggie's family had always referred to as a "gingerbread house".

Maggie and I were lucky enough to have other family members. Our three cats, Rembrandt, Rubens, and Squeaky, moved with us to

Shaftesbury Avenue, but they were already aging cats by then, and one by one they succumbed to the depredation of old age. The last to leave us was Rubens, who was then twenty years old and had to be sent mercifully to his rest. Maggie mourned them all, since they were all characters, each in his or her own way, and we never hesitated to say that they had become members of the family. We were then catless for a little more than a year. Maggie learned that a colleague was serving as a foster parent for kittens that had turned up at the humane society, a role that got the kittens used to the company of people within their first few weeks. Maggie was hooked, and a couple of weeks later she asked me if we could adopt three kittens. One of Maggie's most lovable expressions spread across her face when she was thinking about or cuddling a cat or kitten, and the first kitten arrived at Shaftesbury Avenue soon after. That was Miles, one of the two cats who now own my condo but allow me to live in it.

Miles came to us at age five weeks in a small cardboard box that had been filled with wood shavings. He wasn't sure about his new surroundings at all, and for the first night he stayed in his bed of shavings. On his first morning with us, we found him still nestled in his wood shavings. We gave him some breakfast, but after that the only place he was comfortable was back among his shavings. On his second morning, we found him exploring the downstairs bathroom. He had worked out the purpose of the small litter tray, and he began to creep hesitantly along one wall of the kitchen. But he wouldn't go farther than that. By the third morning, he had taken ownership of the entire house.

The other two kittens arrived together a few days later. They were less hesitant about exploring, perhaps because Miles had already subdued all potential threats. The one thing they learned about and loved immediately was the carpeted stairs. Each of the steps was a little high for a five-week-old kitten to scale at a single bound, but they spent hours struggling up and down the stairs one step at a time, looking like novice but determined rock-face climbers. Within a few days, Miles had developed enough strength to run up the stairs right to the top of the house. This became a habit for him at bedtime, and despite Maggie and me having a head start, Miles always would make it to the bedroom first, in triumph.

Our large bedroom had sliding doors enclosing a closet space all along the south wall of the room, and two of these sliding doors were fitted with full-length mirrors. The first time Miles made it to this bedroom, he found himself confronted by a cat. Another cat! In his house! His tail fluffed up. He arched his back. He took a run at this other cat to try to frighten it. But his opponent was made of tougher stuff, and the scurvy little sod lunged at Miles at the same time. This went on for a few minutes until Miles lost interest. He approached the other cat closely, and they were almost touching noses. I think at that point Miles recognized that the other cat had no scent whatever, and that the whole thing must have been just an odd dream.

It didn't take long for us to learn that a house is an incubator of projects. The two bedrooms on the second floor needed work, and that was our first renovation project. The roof would soon need reshingling, something that gave rise to our second project. The den had floor-to-ceiling bookshelves along the east wall, but we needed more shelf space, so we had that shelving duplicated on the west wall. The stucco on the outside west wall of the house was beginning to crack and spall, and to avoid any serious water inleakage problems, we had that side of the house covered by insulated and anodized metal siding, having the same grey shade as the bricks on the front of the house. That wall was a large expanse, and the first impact of the siding was to cut our heating costs dramatically.

Another large project took shape when we realized that two doors on the ground floor were not closing properly. A home inspector quickly diagnosed the problem: The back half of the house, the portion the previous owner had not had undergirded by a dug-out basement, was resting on large wooden baulks. These baulks were rotting, and the back of the house was shifting and settling slowly. The solution was to extend the basement right to the back of the house. As part of that project, we decided to have a new high-efficiency furnace and a high-efficiency water heater installed and to replace the air-conditioning compressor. Soon our lot was a construction site. The cats watched with trepidation as a fearsome mechanical Martian lumbered about in what had been the back garden, hauling loads of soil from beneath the kitchen. During this work, Maggie set up a camp kitchen in the dining room. Once the excavating was finished, the back of the house was supported on six or eight wood beams. Those beams looked completely inadequate for the job (Maggie referred to them as "toothpicks"), and although the contractor said it was perfectly safe to go into the kitchen to retrieve things, Maggie wouldn't go near the place. Eventually, the concrete-block walls for the new back basement were in place and the toothpicks were removed. Even then, Maggie's first venture into the kitchen was done with the care and uncertainty of someone clinging to the great north face of the Eiger.

In parallel to this major work being undertaken, Maggie and I decided to install a ground-floor toilet between the dining room and the kitchen. My mother often visited us for lunch, and it was becoming harder for her to climb the stairs to the first-floor loo. Maggie tackled this sub-project with gusto. She wanted our new ground-floor loo to have a look that matched the age of the original house. Maggie found a delightful local antiques place called Steptoe and Wife where she unearthed some period lavatory fittings. There was a facsimile toilet bowl, a wall-mounted flush tank, and a flush pull chain having a white porcelain handle on the end that sported the instruction "Pull" in Victorian script. We located a cabinetmaker to construct a wooden toilet seat and a wooden surround for the wall-mounted tank. I asked him to make the surround for the flush tank such that there was space for two standard-sized porcelain tiles to be fitted on the front face of the surround. Steptoe and Wife also had a beautiful sink standing on elegant porcelain legs, something retrieved when an old hotel had had its bathrooms and bedrooms renovated. We found some facsimile taps that looked like gold-plated metal but with white porcelain handles, helpfully labelled "Warm" and "Cold", also in suitably old-style script. The idea of tiles on the front side of the flush tank appealed to Maggie right away. We went off to one of the better tile shops and looked at what was available. Two tile designs caught my attention, and I bought them on the spot. They were wrapped and we took them home.

The work all came to completion. The new ground-floor loo looked stunning. I unwrapped our two tiles and held them up to the tank. The tiles depicted lovely healthy green vegetables and were a perfect fit, so I set about installing them on the tank.

Maggie was watching me, and that was when the penny dropped. She laughed in real pleasure.

"No!" she said. "You can't have pictures of leeks and peas in the toilet!"

It wasn't all that often I was able to slip something like that past

Maggie, and I felt quite proud of myself. The tiles that were mounted eventually showed flowers from an A. A. Milne poem: red geraniums and blue delphiniums. But as long as Maggie and I lived in Shaftesbury Avenue, I noticed, on numerous occasions, Maggie coming out of our ground-floor loo with a smirk on her lips.

We had three more projects at Shaftesbury Avenue.

In the back garden, pathetic patches of grass fought a losing battle to draw sustenance from a thin layer of almost infertile soil. This soil was spread over four or five inches of completely infertile stone chips. The back garden was almost entirely shaded, and we knew what we wanted. The skim of soil and the layer of stone chips were removed, a thick layer of rich soil was spread over the garden, and we then had large, flat, irregular granite slabs laid, leaving enough space around the slabs for flowers and herbs to be planted. Each of these slabs was about three inches thick, two or three square feet in area, and way too heavy for anybody to think about pinching one. We eventually planted hostas (which don't mind the shade), alyssum (which did better than we expected), vinca, some climbing vines along two sides of the wooden fence, and lots of thyme. One of our cats found that thyme tastes quite good in small quantities, and Maggie characterized his work out there as "thyme management". Those granite slabs looked completely beautiful after a rain.

In the front garden, we altered the direction of the path to our front door, having it come in along the front of the house right next to the flower beds instead of diagonally from the corner where Ottawa Street and Shaftesbury Avenue meet. Between this new entranceway and the garden right next to it we had an attractive line of white-painted aluminum railing installed. In spring, the dwarf forsythia (and a little later, the tall poppies) displayed themselves well against that white railing. We also had flower beds installed along the west side of the front garden, the side next to Ottawa Street, where Maggie planted sage, mint, several kinds of scented thyme, lily of the valley, and two spirea bushes. Maggie worked on the front garden most nice weekends, and we both would stop on the way in to do a few minutes of weeding. On the front step, just to the left of the door, we placed two half wine barrels, no longer of use to the winery and picked up for a song. We filled those barrels with a mixture of compost and bagged soil, and Maggie grew chives, rosemary, parsley, and many varieties of small tomatoes. Those tomatoes tasted like candy, but we were never able to use any of them in our cooking; we snacked way too much on them as we went out to work in the morning. As an afterthought, we installed "something" next to the magnolia that bordered the sidewalk on Shaftesbury and onto which our front door looked directly. That "something" was a small and tastefully embellished cast concrete bench that we had found languishing at the back of a garden supplies yard. Maggie and I often sat on that little bench, sipping glasses of wine and seeing the envious or approving glances cast our way by neighbours passing on the sidewalk. Having Maggie seated beside me there on our bench, in the shade, quietly enjoying our wine, was something that took me to a neverland, and it felt wonderful and timeless.

Maggie loved working in the front garden and she took every opportunity to do that. One fine Saturday morning she was working near the sidewalk along Ottawa Street. Without warning, the giant head of a Great Dane came over her shoulder and looked to see what she was doing.

"Oh! Hello!" she said. "And what's your name?"

The dog uttered a gentlemanly woof. We talked to the owner for a while. The dog and owner left, but not before the dog gave Maggie's work one last glance of inspection.

The time in our house was our longest and most prominent experience of the complex idea "home", a notion that recurs in different garb throughout this account.

At this point in our lives, Maggie and I were people acquiring assets. We were in early middle age but remained young at heart, and this likely shielded us from thoughts of what the world might deliver.

My aunts and uncles were aging, and it was at about this time that they began departing. It was solemn, hardly unexpected, and something that not only I had to weather, but that had impacts for Maggie as well since she had grown fond of a number of my relatives. But something happened that struck closer to home, something we weren't prepared for.

On October 25, 1992, we received a telephone call saying that Maggie's mother had died. The call came from Maggie's father, who sounded as though he was only just holding it together. We found out later that Joan had died suddenly of a ruptured aortic aneurysm while napping on her bed in the afternoon. Maggie and I made arrangements immediately to fly back to England. It was a sombre time.

Maggie and her mother had a particular bond. In many ways, they were alike: both were bright, both had a practical view of the world and how to live in it, and both were realists.

Joan had left her affairs entirely in order. She had designated items that she wanted to go to Maggie and Chris and to her daughter-in-law and son-in-law. Maggie received several prized pieces of Joan's jewellery and some elegant items of china. What came to me was something that surprised and delighted me: Joan's set of the novels of Michael Innes. These were books that Joan had read several times and enjoyed, and she remembered them from decades earlier, reminding her of her time in Oxford where Innes (a.k.a. J. I. M. Stewart) was a professor. It was a gift that left me feeling flattered.

In the months after her mother died, Maggie spent a good deal of time with her father. Maggie loved her father even though they had characteristics in common that could lead to clashes. John came from an age when the husband looked after the finances and any-thing technical, while the wife handled everything else to do with the household. Despite that practice, Joan was quite capable at most things. John, on the other hand, was virtually helpless in the kitchen, and Maggie undertook to show him how to prepare a half-dozen simple meals. John had great support from another quarter. His time in the Masons had left him many good friends, and these gentlemen took turns coming to spend a few hours or a day with John for weeks after Joan died. Maggie and I had discussions with various people, working out how we would provide the longer-term assistance to John that we were all sure he would need, and likely sooner than later. On the flight back to Toronto after her mother's funeral, Maggie told me that she worried about her father, and I could tell that she wished we were within easier reach of him.

During that period, Maggie flew to England several times, on each occasion for only a short visit, and during those visits she cooked up a storm and filled John's freezer. The need for that kind of emergency assistance came to an end when John announced, not quite a year after Joan's death, that he was remarrying.

John's second wife, Margaret, was a long-time friend of Joan, some-one she had known from student days. Margaret and John were a good match. They travelled. John moved from Sandpipers to Margaret's house in Worcester. They were happy. That happiness lasted a few years. Then Margaret died of a stroke.

That event knocked the stuffing out of John, something that became clear to Maggie. To an even greater extent than after the death of her mother, our physical distance from John was something that troubled Maggie. Once more, she travelled several times to England to be with her father and to cook for him. That period didn't last long.

We learned that John had been admitted to hospital. It took little time for the backstory to come out. A neighbour had found him lying on the path one night, in a cold rain. He soon developed pneumonia. I have always believed that he simply gave up, that he saw no point in carrying on. I'm not sure what Maggie thought. It was painful, and I tried not to discuss the matter with her. The important thing was to be with Maggie, to grieve with her. We travelled to England after John had died, and the four of us, Denyse and Chris, Maggie and I, undertook the job of clearing out the house where Margaret and John had lived. It was a week of emotionally painful work and eighteen-hour days.

Denyse and Chris and their three children lived in Munich, and though Maggie had cousins in England, without Joan and John to visit, our trips there became less frequent. And both Maggie and I focussed on our lives and our careers in Toronto.

One aspect of our lives in Toronto was a social event that began about that time and carried on for more than twenty years. That was our annual New Year's Eve bash. The people invited to this bash varied slightly from year to year, but there were three couples, apart from Maggie and me, who were the core group.

This annual event began by just five people getting together: our Shaftesbury Avenue neighbours Marg and Tony; a friend of theirs, Harriet, who became one of our good friends as well; and Maggie and me. The first event involving these five people was just an elaborate dinner accompanied by specially chosen wine, a tipsy Auld Lang Syne at midnight, and then an hour or two of conversation to bring in the new year. These events soon expanded to a group of typically ten to fourteen people, and they became themed dinners. That they were such a runaway success was due almost entirely to Maggie, who was a natural chatelaine and very much enjoyed the company of friends.

One of our themed evenings was Spanish, another was Italian, and a third was French. We had a Southern African evening, including dishes from South Africa, Mozambique, Zimbabwe, and a dish that was one of Nelson Mandela's favourites, umngqusho. We had a Woodstock evening. We had a Beatles evening. We had a Northern Ontario evening, and Maggie's imagination was what carried that occasion to success. We found something called birch syrup at the Royal Winter Fair and discovered that a teaspoon of birch syrup would transform steamed carrots. The meat for that evening was what Maggie called ptarmigan. It wasn't real ptarmigan, but a large chicken transformed to a tundra bird using Maggie's special "ptarmigan sauce".

Maggie's delight in these bashes went well beyond the food. We often had matching theme music for the evening, and there was always some special decoration involving wall posters, candles, table mats, partial costumes, and, frequently, strings of tiny coloured lights for a bit of extra frivolity. There was always some kind of quiz, on one occasion involving clues on pieces of paper stuck to walls, mirrors, doors, and windows. Each of those occasions was precious to Maggie because of the pleasure she derived from planning, testing, and serving whatever food combinations we had selected, but also because of the great joy of having good friends, good food, and good wine come together for six or seven wonderful hours.

The New Year's Eve bash was not the only stand-out social event on our calendar. Maggie was a Piscean, as am I, and oddly enough, a good number of Maggie's work colleagues were also Pisceans. So Maggie decided on a Pisces Party, and that became a regular event. Once we had moved to our condo at Market Square, all those occasions continued.

Our move from a house to a condo was an important one. There were good reasons for making the move, but also conflicting considerations. Property prices in Toronto had just begun to take off and extracting the equity from our house was something not to be sniffed at. Against that, we had lived in the house for thirty years, we loved the place, Maggie had produced something close to an English country garden at the corner of Shaftesbury and Ottawa Streets, and any move was bound to feel like abandoning an old friend to make something of a leap into the unknown. Our lovely Shaftesbury house was on four levels, and although that posed no immediate problem, it might become a concern as we grew older. Finding a place on one level made some sort of sense. Finally, there were things about our house that came round every year and took time and effort, such as trimming shrubs and hedges, raking leaves, cleaning out eavestroughs, and clearing ice and snow. Once again, these didn't represent extreme inconveniences but seemed to be things it would be nice to be able to avoid.

At the time, Maggie and I already owned a condo in a modern lowrise building at Shaftesbury Avenue and Yonge Street, located not much more than a hundred metres from our house. We had bought it intending that my mother would live there, close to us, but she went cool on that idea. So we had rented it out for several years. The condo was in the building called The Ports and in many ways it was perfect. All the windows and a balcony there faced east over the tennis courts that were part of the building's amenities and toward the houses in Summerhill. There were larger condo units on the west side of the building, but Yonge Street on that side was noisy. Our unit was a spacious one-bedroom that was generous for one person but would have been too small for two.

When Maggie and I decided to move, we did a great deal of looking around. Our first instinct was to remain in the Summerhill-St. Clair area, which we knew and found livable. But we looked at condos, perhaps thirty-five in total, over a large area of midtown and downtown. There were six or seven in the immediate Yonge-Summerhill area, but all had more disadvantages than advantages. We viewed more than a dozen condos in the Yonge-Eglinton area, ranging from Avenue Road to Mount Pleasant. We looked at another dozen or so along the waterfront, all the way from the Humber to Leslie Street. A lasting impression from all that searching was that new condos could be something of a joke. A tiny alcove with a desk in it qualified as a "study". The second bedrooms in many two-bedroom units were not much more than glorified broom closets. Considered relative to one another, the rooms in many new condos were often all out of proportion: a dining room might seat eight people, but in the tiny kitchen, one would have trouble preparing a meal for more than three. This was all in the late summer and early autumn of 2004.

In October of 2004, we sold our condo in The Ports building. We continued to look at condos for sale, but it was becoming disheartening. Late in December, we viewed Suite 503 at 35 Church Street in the Market Square complex. The place badly needed updating, but its bones were good. We asked our agent about putting in an offer. She proposed doing so early in January. Maggie and I insisted on making an offer before the end of the year, and on December 26 we did so. It was slightly low, but not insultingly so, and we asked our agent to tell the sellers that the offer was good for only three days.

The unit had been on the market for some time, and during the last week of the year, nobody was buying, since all attention was focussed on Christmas. One counteroffer by the sellers came back, we made a further offer, and everyone signed off. Maggie and I had become the owners of a condo in Market Square.

For various reasons, we decided not to move right away. "Not right away" turned out to be almost eight years later, and we moved to our condo in September 2012, a few months after I retired. One of those eight years was taken up by renovation.

It would take a good many words to describe Maggie's efforts in planning our condo renovation and tracking its progress. She had everything in a spiral-bound notebook: what we wanted to do in each room, which walls we wanted taken down or relocated, how we would turn the kitchen from a gloomy space enclosed on all sides to a bright and attractive galley kitchen, choices for the kitchen cabinets and working surfaces (including a special dough-kneading surface for my breads), cupboard space, appliances, bathroom fittings, walk-in closet modifications, and having all the traditional unattractive doors replaced by sliding frosted-glass doors. I lost track of how many lighting, appliance, plumbing, tiling, flooring, and contractors' showrooms we visited. But Maggie had it all in her notebook. In the end, everything was selected, renovations began, and we visited our work in progress regularly.

Before our furniture, books, china, and cooking pots were moved, Maggie and I toured our completed new home. I knew that Maggie still regretted not having a garden, but her eyes did sparkle during that tour, and I knew we would be quite happy here.

Maggie's detailed planning paid off. In September 2012, everything was finished and it looked fantastic. Gone was the tired look that dated back to 1981 when the building was constructed: the white shag floor rug that had turned a depressing grey after more than thirty years' use; the ugly, bulbous jacuzzi bathtub; the cut-rate kitchen cabinets that must have been cheap even in 1980; the peeling paint; and the unimaginative lighting. Our renovations were a major physical adaptation but they weren't the only change to affect our living arrangements, nor even the most important. We found that many people in the Market Square condo buildings soon became friends. This was something we didn't expect. And we were surprised and delighted to see that acquiring these new acquaintances produced a considerable positive reorientation in our social lives. We found that our condo unit and our lives became a minor centre of social activity in our building.

Since Market Square is in the St. Lawrence district, the identification of August 10 as St. Lawrence's feast day suggested another social occasion: a St. Lawrence Party on or close to August 10 each year. This turned out to be a cracking success, partly because of Maggie's enthusiasm and the spread of foods she prepared and partly because our Market Square neighbours turned out in force and made it a success. Typical of the level of participation and enjoyment was the comment made by our resident bishop on his arrival at his first St. Lawrence Party. He looked at the food arrayed on the tables and wanted to know where the roast meat was. The reference was lost on few people, St. Lawrence having been martyred by being roasted on a grid iron.

Maggie and I now had a very presentable living space, what one friend referred to as "the million-dollar condo" — long before that was an accurate description of what became an actual reality. Maggie loved the kitchen, which had more cupboard and drawer space than our house on Shaftesbury. She also loved the long living-dining area, which turned out to be an ideal entertaining space, good for our Pisces and St. Lawrence parties, since forty or more people could mingle comfortably in that space, and perfect for our New Year's Eve parties.

The move to our condo at 35 Church Street was the last move Maggie and I made. After retiring in 2012, I embarked on a second career as an author. Maggie's ten years from 2012 included probably the most rewarding period of her working life. During that period, we also travelled quite a bit. It isn't easy to capture what our travels meant. But they involved family, discovery, history, friends, old haunts, new vistas, food, wine, and so much else, all blended into a rich and inviting palette. The best I can do here is to provide some highlights.

CHAPTER 12

THE PALETTE OF OUR TRAVELS

Apart from travelling for business, Maggie and I often made trips chiefly to visit family and friends in Europe and elsewhere in Canada. There were many trips to England. Once Chris's work had taken him to Germany full time, we visited Denyse and Chris in Munich about five times. Later, Chris followed his project to France, and we visited them there quite a few times. Our last trip to Provence together was in March 2020.

Maggie travelled a little bit on her own for pleasure, but not much. I travelled much more on my own for pleasure, and I have always recognized that Maggie never raised any objections to that. In fact, she encouraged it. Most of that travel was for bicycle trips in Germany with my German cycling friend, Ralf. I came to know Ralf through one of our friends here in Toronto, Liz, whose sister was Ralf's wife.

England

My first life-changing trips to England (and Europe) have been recounted already in some detail. After the deaths of Maggie's parents, our trips to England focussed elsewhere. Maggie had a long-standing friend, Sue, who lives in York, and we visited there several times. Trips to York were always much more than just visiting friends since there are any number of historic sites in that area. On one trip, Maggie and I stumbled upon a replica RAF base, complete with the sounds of Spitfires and Lancasters passing overhead, control-tower conversations, and displays of all kinds of memorabilia. On that same trip, we stopped at RAF Coningsby where the only operational Lancaster in Britain has its home base, and where about a dozen airworthy Spitfires are located. This had particular meaning for me since Maggie had bought me a ride in the Canadian Lancaster for my sixtieth birthday. That plane flies out of Mount Hope airfield near Hamilton where its hangar at the Canadian Warplane Heritage Museum is located. On the same trip, we toured the Railway Museum in York and a Roman staging camp for legions on the march up and down that part of England.

On other trips to the southern part of England, we very much enjoyed the Tank Museum at Bovington in Dorset and the Royal Signals Museum at Blandford. We also visited the grave of T. E. Lawrence (of Arabia) at St. Nicholas Church in Moreton and his home in Clouds Hill, all these places also in Dorset. These were combined with visits to see Maggie's cousin Jeffrey at Broadstone. Visits of a less historic bent involved a gorgeous B&B near Lulworth, to which Maggie was attracted right away by a line on its website that described it as within "stumbling distance from the pub". Our stays at that B&B necessarily meant trips to Lulworth Cove and to a rock formation on the coast known as Durdle Door, a drive over the Purbeck Hills, and stops at Weymouth, Wareham, Corfe Castle, Portland Bill, and Chesil Beach.

Even if Maggie and I had been granted another twenty-five years, we wouldn't have been able do more than just scratch the surface of what remains.

Italy

During our time in Vienna, Maggie and I made the easy hop to places in Northern Italy. We went to Venice once by train and once in our car. In a separate trip, we crossed the Alps through the Brenner Pass, dropped down into Bolzano, then descended the lovely Adige Valley to spots around Lake Garda. We were looking for scenery, good food, and good wine, and we found all three.

In approximately 2014, Ralf and I did a bicycle trip from Bolzano to Venice, and at the same time Maggie and her friend Liz flew to Rome and took the fast train to Venice, where we all met. Liz had never been to Venice, and Maggie insisted that she had to visit at least once. After a few days in Venice, Ralf made his way back to his home in Rommelhausen, while Maggie, Liz, and I took the train to Florence to do some rubber necking and added a side trip to Pisa. I then made my way back to Rommelhausen for a few days, while Maggie and Liz returned to Rome for a few days. The three of us arrived back in Toronto soon after that and had a debriefing, seasoned travellers comparing notes over a bottle of wine.

Much later, Maggie and I travelled to Genoa where I collected material for one of my novels, *Sicilian Refuge.* Further material for that novel was collected in Sicily, and Maggie and I and our good friend Dawn spent a memorable time there.

Maggie knew Italy from her youth since she worked as an au pair in Pisa and Rome for a good part of a year between secondary school and university. That was definitely before my appearance on the scene, but I know from what Maggie told me that her time in Italy then was formative.

SOUTH AFRICA

From Vienna, we also took advantage of low airfares to South Africa. We had made the acquaintance of a South African, Jan, who had been sent to North America in 1977 to study practices in the electricity industry (the industry in which he was employed in South Africa). Jan's first stop was Toronto, and I had been asked to squire him around during his stay. Maggie and I got along well with Jan practically from the first moment, and he and I kept in touch from then on. When we found that flights from Vienna to Johannesburg were too low to pass up, I contacted Jan. He became excited at the prospect right away and insisted that we come.

Being shown around Johannesburg, Cape Town, Kruger Park, and seeing for ourselves Kipling's "great grey-green greasy Limpopo River" was a treat. We saw elephants in the wild, lions resting on the cool paved road in the early morning, the Drakensberg Mountains, Table Mountain, and much more. We rented a caravan and drove east through the veldt from Johannesburg, dropping down to the coast at Durban through the Valley of a Thousand Hills. We spent time with the parents of Maggie's Vienna colleague Frances in a sugar plantation at Umhlanga Rocks. The rest of the time we stayed with Jan in his house in Sandton, south of Pretoria, where we enjoyed great food and wine and the company of Jan's housekeeper, Christina; and where Maggie met some ants.

Christina spoke no English but in typical fashion, Maggie was able to communicate with her easily. Christina enjoyed putting on African music and then swaying through Jan's house as she cleaned it. We also convinced her to cook us some of her staple food, which was something called mealies, a heavy starchy base over which she poured a thick spicy vegetable sauce. We learned as well that Christina was both fearless and greatly fearful. Her fearlessness led her to beat to death a spitting cobra that she came across in Jan's walled garden. This snake attacks anything it considers an enemy by squirting venom at the enemy's eyes, and it has deadly accurate aim at anything up to twelve feet. But Christina was terrified of spiders and would leap onto a chair screaming at the sight of even the smallest harmless spider.

Maggie met the ants one morning in the bathroom. She noticed movement next to the window and realized that it was a column of small ants moving vertically along the wall in both directions. Curious to know where they were going, she followed their path along the floor, behind the toilet, and then farther along the floor on the other side. It wasn't clear how they got past the toilet, where she was seated, but she soon found out. Standing up quickly she could see that they were climbing the pedestal of the toilet bowl then crossing a couple of inches behind where her bum had been. Jan assured us both that the ants were harmless, but Maggie spent as little time as possible on the loo for the rest of our visit.

Australia

Maggie and I made two trips to Australia in the early 1990s, and in both cases, we flew to Sydney. Also, in both cases, we went because Maggie had been invited to a conference each time. I went along to carry the bags and drive, but I also submitted an abstract for a paper at the first conference. The paper was entitled "The Care and Feeding of Librarians" and was written from the point of view of a library user. Me. To my surprise, it was accepted. Delivering the paper was a blast. Apart from that, Maggie and I spent time with some of her Australian colleagues, and I even had a game of tennis with one of them under a stand of huge blue gum trees. There was a kookaburra somewhere up in those trees, and he burst out laughing at intervals. Probably at my serve.

I lost. Of course.

In Sydney, we stayed at a lovely hotel called The Russell Hotel, right opposite Circular Quay. It was an exquisite little place that had only about ten rooms, but each room was decorated following a different Australian theme. For breakfast each morning, there was orange juice from oranges that had been brought in that morning from Parramatta. Just outside the entrance to the hotel, there were two pepper trees, and going out into Sydney each morning, we walked through the most gorgeous waft of pepper aroma.

We saw a good deal of Sydney, and we also visited two people we had worked with at the UN in Vienna. One was a woman in the office where I worked but who also got to know Maggie well. She was in Australia because her husband had been posted there with his company. It confirmed our belief that there really is something deliciously snobby about meeting one's friends on the other side of the world.

The second person we met was Hans, a guy I had worked with only occasionally. He was Dutch but had adopted Australia as his home, and he had gone back there after his term in Vienna was finished. We met him in a pub where he introduced us to a whole gaggle of Aussies, and that was a tremendously enjoyable evening. Maggie knew him reasonably well because he was the right-hand man to her boss's boss. In typical Maggie fashion, she had got to know her boss's boss well because they attended the same German class, and we ended up going out to lunch with him and his wife quite a few times. The Australian pub where we met Hans and his mates had an enlarged copy of Kipling's poem "If" on the wall, and Maggie and I stole the show by reciting the poem without looking at that wall.

During that trip, we were having dinner one night at an outdoor restaurant in Sydney. There was a couple at an adjoining table, and the man seemed to be paying a lot of attention to us. I had no idea who he was. But he came over and asked if we were from England or Canada, and of course Maggie said "yes". He wanted to know what I did for a living, and he seemed nice enough, so I told him. He then asked me if I knew someone called Norm S. I did and I said so.

The short version of this is that Norm S. had been at their wedding many years earlier (best man, if I remember correctly), but they had lost contact. He asked me if I would pass their contact information to Norm. When I got back to Canada I did that and soon got notes of thanks from both of them. Somehow, I have the feeling that this wouldn't have happened if Maggie had not been with me. Things, good things, happened when she was around.

During our second trip a few years later, we rented a car and drove from Sydney to Melbourne on an inland route. The conference on that occasion was in Melbourne, but the trip there allowed Maggie to see something she had always wanted to see: some of the features of the great Snowy Mountains project. We spent time looking at one of the lakes that project had generated, Lake Jindabyne. It seemed to cast a spell on Maggie. We then returned to Sydney via the coastal route, and we visited far too many vineyards along both legs of that trip. We ended up having way too many bottles of wine, sherry, and port, and somehow we got through enough of them in a marathon swilling session. We packed the remaining bottles into our luggage and even thought of tossing some clothes to make room. I remember that trip very fondly, and almost everything about it emphasized the fact that life with Maggie was never boring.

New Zealand

Maggie and I made one trip to New Zealand to attend the wedding of one of my work colleagues, Dave, who came to Canada from England on a secondment. He was engaged to a New Zealand veterinary, but at the end of his year, they decided they would make their home in New Zealand. We received an invitation to their wedding at the same time as a blurb came to us from Air Canada saying that we should use our air miles to avoid losing them. We asked for tickets to New Zealand,

and to our astonishment we were offered them. Two return flights to New Zealand for $300 was impossible to turn down.

I rented a car, and before and after the wedding, we did some touring on the southern half of South Island. We visited the historic gold-mining settlement of Arrowtown, spent some time in Queenstown, and made our way to Invercargill on the southern tip of South Island, where Maggie charmed a lovely young Turkish man, Mustafa, by telling him that he made the best coffee in Invercargill.

The scenery was simply astonishing, and we stayed at a B&B where the host found kindred spirits in both of us as jokers.

CALIFORNIA

When Maggie worked as the main representative in Canada for Dialog, she was obliged to go to California each year for a meeting of all the international representatives. She looked forward to meeting her Mexican, Brazilian, Chilean, Australian, and other counterparts, but the meetings themselves tended to be rah-rah sessions to pump up enthusiasm.

I accompanied Maggie on a few of these trips, and she looked forward to finishing up the business gatherings in Palo Alto and touring nearby areas. We spent an interesting few days in the Napa and Sonoma Valleys. On one occasion, we spent quite a bit of time in San Francisco. Another time, when one of Maggie's colleagues, Louise, went to California as well, we enjoyed a trip to the south of San Francisco, spent time flopped on a beach, had some excellent meals and wine, and took in the countryside around Carmel. During these trips, we met many people and had some fascinating conversations.

However, one thing struck us forcefully. Palo Alto is likely one of the wealthiest communities in the world, and the main drag running through it is El Camino Real. Walking just a few blocks to the east of El Camino Real, we came across a Black woman dragging her laundry along the street to a laundromat. She wore no shoes. She was evidently almost indigent, and it was clear that her poverty-stricken status wasn't an exception. It seemed that this image didn't disturb any of the other people in the street, but Maggie and I both felt uncomfortable.

I suppose everyone becomes accustomed to what is around them. But to us it all seemed somewhat unreal.

FRANCE

Maggie and I visited France many times. In 1985, we travelled to the South of France with two friends, Debbie and Pete, and did what seemed to be the impossible: We visited spots pretty much from Monaco to Bordeaux, in a single car, over a period of a little more than two weeks, and we never had an argument. For that trip, each person was asked to select one thing they wanted to see, and we agreed that we would all go to each person's choice, no objections and no questions.

Maggie chose the Pont du Gard. Pete selected the Marine Museum in Monaco. Debbie wanted to see the wild white horses in the Camargue. And I opted for a grand wine chateau in Bordeaux. My selection was possible because, at that time, my sister worked for the large international wine-and-spirits company that owned Chateau Loudenne as its flagship French operation, and she was able to arrange a visit for the four of us.

It was an excellent holiday. Everything clicked. The Pont du Gard was stunning and was everything that Maggie had expected. The Marine Museum was good. We saw some white horses in the Camargue, but they were in the distance, and not, as many postcards indicated, ridden through the surf by naked blonde French maidens. The wine chateau took the prize, however. As we drove up the long tree-lined avenue to the chateau itself, we could see flagpoles at the main entrance flying the Swedish and Canadian flags. I began to wonder what had been organized and whether I would be turned away for not bringing a tux.

A butler greeted us and showed us where to park. We were shown to our sumptuous rooms, and before leaving us, the butler asked if we would like gin and tonic to enjoy in our baths. It seemed like "yes" was the only sensible answer.

That afternoon, we had a wine tasting in the chateau's tasting room where we met an older gentleman who was touring the region buying wine for various London clubs. He was utterly charming, and it seemed that what he didn't know about wine wasn't worth knowing.

Back in our rooms late that afternoon, we found that we were invited to dinner in one of the chateau's intimate dining rooms, the invitation making it clear that everything was entirely informal. The chatelaine was an English woman and she was very gracious. We were apparently the only overnight guests, so we asked if we could do the entertaining, suggesting that the chatelaine might like to have a relaxed evening for a change. She smiled and said okay. But we found that there really was little to do. However, Pete and I found the CD collection, chose some music, and settled in.

It was an evening to remember. Maggie contributed more than her share to the scintillating conversation. Pete and I took on the role of wine stewards, pouring wine from the selections that had been lined up for the evening. The meal was prepared and served by the kitchen staff — sand dabs from the Gironde to start, magret de canard for the main course, and crème brûlée for dessert. Needless to say, there was nothing about the meal that wasn't perfect.

On that same trip, we wanted to visit a decent winery in the Chateauneuf-du-Pape region. We pulled into one that we just happened to notice, Chateau Mousset. It turned out to be well known and, as they would say in France, *une bonne cave*. It was late in the day, and we were the only visitors, so we had the full attention of the man behind the tasting bar. And we tasted. And we bought quite a few bottles.

To one side of the tasting room was a large table, and on that table slept a self-assured black cat whose name we learned was Moïse, or Moses in English. Moïse stirred himself to open one eye and look at us disdainfully but evidently decided that we weren't worth any more trouble than that. However, the table, according to the man who had served us, had been used by Alphonse Daudet to write *Lettres de mon Moulin*, and the table had come from Daudet's windmill. This little tidbit inspired one of my short stories, "Le Chat Moïse".

A memorable visit to France occurred in 2000 when we met Maggie's twin brother, Chris, and his wife and family in Tours for Maggie's and Chris's fiftieth birthday. We did some local touring. We had some excellent meals. But we probably spent a disproportionate time dropping into wineries to do some tasting. Over the years, Maggie and I have tasted wine on four continents and in twelve countries, and we both loved talking to the vintners and hearing their stories. During the visit to Tours, we enjoyed the care and attention and the patience shown by the people leading us through tastings. They explained the wines and their origins with care, in French that was clear and spoken slowly.

On the way from one vineyard to another, we noticed a restaurant set in a space hollowed out of a chalk bank. The chef was outside, and we arranged a time to turn up that evening for dinner. That was a delightful evening. Little lights were placed in tiny alcoves cut into the chalk walls inside the restaurant. It hardly needs saying that the food was excellent. In fact, the whole evening is something I still remember in some detail.

But by far, the greatest number of visits Maggie and I made to France were to visit her brother where he and Denyse still live, in the village of Saint-Paul-lez-Durance, about forty kilometres northeast of Aix-en-Provence. The first time we visited, Maggie toured the house and garden and said to me afterward, "I'm green." I felt guilty yet again about taking Maggie away from Europe. On subsequent visits, we did all the things one is expected to do. We visited village markets, saw the gorgeous lavender fields near Valensole, sat nursing drinks in Aix-en-Provence while we watched people shop in the city's markets, visited the coast at Cassis, spent a day in the exquisite town of Saint-Rémy-de-Provence, engaged in banter with Didier in his shop and restaurant in St. Paul (a place sporting the name "Le Boeuf Chantant"), and perhaps most important, sat around the pool drinking pastis. Maggie loved those visits. And some of her ashes are scattered around an olive tree behind Chris's house there.

GERMANY

While I visited Germany many times to do bicycle trips with my German friend Ralf, Maggie accompanied me on those trips less often. From Vienna, we travelled to Munich a number of times for long weekends. Those trips were most pleasant, and we always found Munich to be an interesting and vibrant city.

For ten years, Maggie's brother and his wife and family lived in a suburb of Munich called Neubiberg. Chris was there because the international fusion project where he worked had moved there from England. We visited Chris and his family there about five times; we were always welcomed and we enjoyed every visit.

Maggie and I also spent some time in Rommelhausen (Limeshain) where Ralf lives. At that time, Ralf's now late wife, Anne, was present. The sights around Rommelhausen are low key, but like almost everywhere in Europe, there is a depth of history there that can be explored with little effort. Maggie and I also enjoyed German cuisine, despite the scepticism some people have that such a thing exists. It does exist, and at its best, it is very fine.

CANADA

Maggie travelled to many parts of Canada as part of her work for Dialog. This included locations in Newfoundland, Nova Scotia, Ontario, Manitoba, Alberta, British Columbia, and one trip to the Yukon.

Newfoundland was always a visually entertaining place full of friendly natives. We visited Cape Spear, the most easterly point of North America, on a day when a driving cold wind off the Atlantic made our faces numb in just a few minutes. We went up Signal Hill. We stayed in the Battery Hotel, which had a dramatic view out over the harbour. The colourful streets of St. John's were always inviting, and we went to the almost impossibly attractive settlement of Quidi Vidi for a superb meal at The Flake House. We were screeched in. We kissed a cod. We visited the seal enclosure of Memorial University where several seals clearly wondered who we were and what we were doing. It was easy to see that Maggie enjoyed every aspect of Newfoundland.

Maggie and I both felt that Nova Scotia was almost a second home in Canada. Maggie was a sessional lecturer at Dalhousie University for a term, but before that, we had spent time in Halifax and places along the coast down to Lunenburg. Halifax always seemed to us a place of mystery. One of my uncles had served on a destroyer escorting convoys from Halifax to Murmansk during the Second World War. My father had left for Europe during that war from Pier 21, which now houses the superb Canadian Museum of Immigration. I had enjoyed the books of Thomas Raddall, especially *Halifax: Warden of the North*. Maggie and I both felt like we were in another world when we saw banks of fog rolling into the old part of Halifax from the harbour, turning the city into a clutch of nebulous shapes punctuated by cones of light clinging to the street lamps. We never missed the chance of a fish dinner at McKelvie's, and Maggie had to restrain me from stopping at every inviting spot along the waterfront for yet another pint of local brew. During several of these trips, I collected material for my novel *Rolls*, and although Maggie felt that it wasn't my best effort, she gave it a passing grade anyway.

Images of Maggie in places across Canada crowd into my mind's eye. But they are too numerous to describe. All I can say is that Maggie's enthusiasm for having new experiences shines into my being from each of these images. How I wish we could have had time to do more.

Belgium

Maggie and I took our first holiday together in Belgium in 1972. We wanted to stay in Bruges but settled for Ghent because it was quite a bit cheaper. We had ten-day rail passes, and we used them to the maximum.

The experience of that first holiday was novel for both of us. We were a modest version of *A Man and a Woman*, watching our expenditures but, at the same time, enjoying the lovely buildings, the walks along the country canals near Bruges, the meals of fish, Flemish beef, many crepes, and the enjoyment of each other's company at all levels.

In some ways, our Belgian holiday remained the best in our minds, partly because it was the first time we travelled together, but perhaps also because the "man and woman" theme was somehow new and important, and it bonded us together in such a strong and intimate way.

CHAPTER 13

MAGGIE REACHING THE SUMMIT

Maggie's long, fascinating, productive, and successful working career was, to me, simply astonishing and is the stuff that dreams are made of. From her earliest position at Aslib to SVP and on to her first consulting company job in Toronto, she moved easily through positions at the UN in Vienna. Then it was back to Canada, where she rejoined the management consulting field. There followed a long stint in the chemical industry, something that was formative for everything that followed: a two-year project during which she started up the IntelliSearch operation at the Toronto Public Library and then a long period at Micromedia. The Micromedia work was where Maggie began to draw seriously on the great wealth of expertise she had developed over the previous twenty years. From Micromedia, Maggie moved into a series of positions in which she developed practically unequalled capability in the area of trade and export.

At this point, I will tell in more detail the story of Maggie reaching the peak in her career. It was during this time, following her position at Micromedia, that she really strove to her vocational summit. But before going there, I want to talk a bit about my doubts on whether a move to Canada was the best thing for Maggie to have done. If it wasn't the best thing, then it was a problem to be laid at my feet.

It isn't that Maggie ever seemed to feel disadvantaged. In fact, she flourished professionally in Canada. My doubts arose from the thought that Maggie had been removed from her cultural surroundings. We were happy in Toronto. The move to Vienna was challenging but it turned out to be an adventure in every sense and a strongly positive experience. Back in Toronto, the sailing quickly became smooth again. Between us, we earned good money. With very few exceptions, we had jobs that met the three main criteria for acceptability (good bosses and work colleagues, interesting work, good pay), we had good friends and we settled into welcoming local communities. But on other levels, many elements of life in Canada did not match their counterparts in England. That was evident to me, and I think that Maggie felt it even more.

I have talked to many people about life in a country one might not consider one's own, about the differences in national, social, and cultural backdrops, about the reasons why different people can see their home countries through very different lenses, and how different people can see life in another country as an adventure, an escape, or maybe a prison. For Maggie, I think that life and work in Canada was mostly an adventure. She made many friends here, but then she always made friends no matter where she was. Maggie was not a snob by any means, but I know that there were things she missed, things that were in some way "English". Maggie said more than once that it is doubtful she could have had a career in England as varied and interesting as her career in Canada. But I'm convinced that I could have done much more so that Maggie (so that *we*) could spend months at a time each year somewhere in England, starting many years ago. In these sorts of discussions, one can count on hearing the old chestnut at some point: "Home is where the heart is". This has always seemed to me to be referring to one place, but the heart can long to be in more than one place. And that can give rise to turmoil and some feelings of alienation, so that happiness itself can appear to be something of a paradox.

After leaving Micromedia, Maggie moved through what was, by comparison to what had gone before, a somewhat messy interregnum on the way to her last major professional role. That role was, I believe, her most fulfilling one, and it brought together almost everything she had learned in previous jobs as well as adding a great deal more.

Maggie had become interested in trade. Specifically, she was interested in helping entrepreneurs and small businesses become successful as flourishing exporters wherever export opportunities arose. She took on the job of teaching course modules for the Forum for International Trade Training (FITT), and this drew her into the large field of how to be a successful exporter. Throughout her career, Maggie had excellent traction from her outstanding abilities as an information researcher; she could find information where others didn't even know how to begin. Maggie's understanding of what was essential for the operation of successful small businesses had its origin in her experience in a library operating within a larger corporate context. That understanding was given depth by Maggie's always intense interest in the variety of opportunities and the challenges faced by small independent businesses. Putting all these things together gave Maggie a unique focus as her interest in trade deepened. That experience and those abilities served her well in constructing her FITT course modules.

The FITT courses gave Maggie an increasing profile among people operating small businesses, and companies interested in being successful exporters or opening new export avenues. Export involves paperwork, and the paperwork varies from country to country. Failing to get the paperwork right can mean that an export shipment can be held at some customs barrier, a fatal situation for anything perishable. Small businesses were sometimes reluctant to pay for services that would smooth the passage of exported goods across borders, and Maggie could see a role for herself in providing guidance to those individuals who wanted to go it alone.

In addition to her paid employment throughout her career, Maggie was active on the conference circuit, and she would regularly submit abstracts to try for a slot in whatever conference struck her fancy. This kept her in contact with the very wide range of people she knew throughout the industry, and she was often flying off to a conference in Ottawa, Halifax, Edmonton, or Vancouver.

It was almost a natural follow-on from her FITT teaching for Maggie to accept a job with the City of Toronto in an area that focussed on exports, since there are many small companies in Toronto, and their success was good for everyone. So having the City help to ensure that success made a lot of sense. The bureaucracy turned out to be a considerable disappointment, however. Maggie struggled along in that position for several years. I could see the frustration and disillusionment on her face.

One day, I said to Maggie: "Just resign. We don't need the money. Go look for something that you'll really like doing."

After a few days' thought, Maggie did hand in her resignation. Her relief was palpable. She thought she would take a short break from everything, but the world had other plans.

In the mid-1990s, the federal government created Regional Trade Networks (RTN) in each province across the country. The RTNs brought together all relevant federal and provincial trade partners as a way to coordinate those programmes aimed at helping Canadian businesses identify and take advantage of emerging international export opportunities. Ontario's RTN was known as the Canada Ontario Export Forum (COEF). By early 2000, though, COEF was in need of a facelift both in terms of how it funded its activities and resources and how it delivered timely export assistance to businesses across the province. As part of the facelift, steps were taken to hire a secretariat to manage, administer, and run operations and develop and deliver export seminars. Given Maggie's work with FITT, along with her previous role with the City of Toronto and her strong background in analytical research and information mining, she was a natural fit to take on the role as COEF Secretariat.

Maggie's work with COEF was possibly the most rewarding element of her working life. As part of her responsibilities, she worked closely with both her provincial and federal trade partners to research, identify, and deliver trade information and seminars that met the needs of Ontario exporters. As a somewhat virtual organization, COEF had a fluctuating membership of around twenty partners (including a steering committee of six federal and provincial departments) engaged in various levels of export development. Managing expectations would be a major responsibility as well as a challenge — a bit like herding cats. As secretariat, Maggie primarily reported to two programme managers within the provincial and federal governments. It was through this partnership that Maggie developed a strong working relationship, as well as a close personal friendship, with her provincial counterpart,

Debbie. For over fifteen years, they worked closely together to build up the awareness and the effectiveness of COEF and to expand the range of programmes and services it offered.

Early on in her new role, Maggie undertook work that formed the basis for COEF's ultimate success. The elements of Maggie's work were as follows: to pull together a comprehensive list of all the federal, provincial and other export programmes and services; to develop a database of potential Ontario exporters; and to develop a budget and business plan for all the activities that COEF would undertake. It was clear early on in Maggie's research that there were dozens of government programmes available to help Ontario exporters, but the means to have them operate in an integrated way was missing. Maggie's earlier career positions prepared her well for this new role, and the results of her research flowed naturally into the many seminars she developed and delivered across the province.

The database of Ontario exporters that Maggie developed became a very useful tool to identify companies that were new potential exporters and also those that were more seasoned. In turn, this information provided a better lens to tailor seminar content to different audiences. As well as allowing companies to be identified, the database allowed Maggie and Debbie to determine which sort of seminar would be best suited to which companies in which parts of the province. It was a complex logistical situation, but just the sort of problem Maggie loved to tackle.

It's hard for me to express the degree of enjoyment and satisfaction Maggie derived from this work. She was often bubbling over enthusiastically on how a meeting had gone, the amount of follow-up she received, and even the sometimes long discussions she had had with participants following the meeting, people who really had been fired up and wanted more. The presentations were rarely the same since each meeting involved different small businesses, which were generating different products, delivering to different customers, and exporting to different locations and sometimes under quite different rules. Maggie became an expert on all aspects of international trade and the finer points to be appreciated by small businesses interested in exporting their products or services. She would spend long hours digging out material for a new or modified presentation, formulating responses to follow-up questions, or providing further detail to businesses having more specific questions. Maggie was always generous with her time and with her knowledge. She was able to work quickly while making very few mistakes, and I think the key to this was her ability to see to the heart of a question or problem, to recognize what was important, and to dig out exactly the information needed to provide answers.

By 2016, Maggie and Debbie had criss-crossed the province as a tag-team delivering many seminars to businesses large and small. Though Maggie still enjoyed her work — especially the outreach she did across the province, she started to muse about wrapping up her role as the secretariat. As well, Debbie also had plans to retire later that year. Deep down, I suspect they both realized that COEF wouldn't be the same without the two of them working together, something that had been a long, rewarding, and fun-filled partnership. So they both made the decision to bow out and leave the work in others' hands. Sadly, when Maggie and Debbie left the scene, the skills, knowledge, passion, and commitment that they both brought to their roles left with them. The many presentations per month that Maggie and Debbie had delivered dwindled to a trickle and soon dried up completely.

Maggie regretted the passing of this work, but she had derived enormous satisfaction from applying to it all the skills she had acquired over a long career. Following the end of her COEF work, Maggie directed her effort at consulting, although she didn't want to make it a full-time activity. There were other things she was interested in and an important activity and focus here was professional activities and volunteering.

Maggie had always volunteered her time selflessly. She fulfilled roles within the information community over decades while accepting no payment. She always attended conferences: to present papers, to engage in discussion and debate, and for the chance to meet her many contacts socially, something she enjoyed greatly. Maggie also had something of an undefined status within the information world. She did not have what is accepted as the calling card for full unquestioned entry to all areas of the library world: the MLS, or Master of Library Science post-graduate degree. This didn't stop her for a minute; she carried on doing whatever she felt needed to be done. And in 1999, Maggie was presented the Award for Special Librarianship in Canada, a distinction made annually by the Canadian Association of Special Libraries and Information Services, an organization that, sadly, no longer exists. The citation on Maggie's award is "In recognition of her outstanding contributions to our profession". I attended the meeting when she was presented her award, and the only person prouder than me was Maggie. Proud, but humble at the same time, someone loved by so many of her colleagues.

Maggie took a great and active interest in young people in her profession. She wanted young people not to be timorous. She wanted them to try things, and she spent a lot of time and effort explaining why many tasks and activities that might look difficult or daunting were basically not that at all. Maggie was involved in something called first timers' breakfasts. This was straightforward. Young people attending a conference for the first time, whether they were presenting a paper or not, were teamed up with people like Maggie — older, more experienced, and outgoing — who would meet and talk to these young people at a pre-session breakfast. From there, the conversation would go wherever made sense, but the young person had made a contact and had gone away to their session reassured. Maggie was also involved in an informal sort of business mentoring for young people. Sometimes this would mean going through the details of the economics of running a library. Sometimes Maggie would offer to review and discuss a draft paper. Sometimes Maggie would get together with a group of young people learning the ropes on how to organize and run a committee, how to lead a work or discussion group, how to keep a discussion on track diplomatically, or something as mundane as how to draft meeting minutes that could help move a discussion forward.

Maggie was also a standard bearer for library technicians, without whom libraries would not be able to function. Maggie was a member of at least three associations of library technicians: OALT (Ontario Association of Library Technicians), APLA (Atlantic Provinces Library Association), and ALTA (Association of Library Technicians of Alberta). These were groups of women almost exclusively. Maggie attended their annual meetings whenever she could, either by piggybacking on an existing business trip or just shelling out the money for the flight herself. These meetings were hardly tame affairs. I attended a number of them and found them to be occasions when all the stops frequently were pulled out. I think I never did attend any of the APLA meetings, obviously a serious failing on my part, based on what happened at OALT and ALTA meetings.

As for the annual meetings of any group, the business was conducted soberly, but once that was out of the way, the technicians hit the "Enjoy" button and put the accelerator to the floor. The meetings turned into full-on parties.

The OALT meetings always ended in a boozy rendition, in several keys at the same time, of the song "Wasn't That a Party". And they would sing the lyrics at full throat. Needless to say, Maggie was right in the middle of it all, her trademark irresistible smile at full wattage.

I attended one meeting of ALTA. It was held outside in the summer, I think in Red Deer, and it involved a barbecue. I followed Maggie's lead, grabbed a plate, and joined the queue. During the wait, I spent my time just looking around. There was no point in trying to talk to Maggie. She was being greeted and hailed from all sides, in most cases by people I didn't know. We arrived at the serving hatch. Bear in mind that the attendees at this meeting, once again almost all women, were from cattle country. Many of them were tall and they all had healthy appetites. Which explained why each of us was delivered two largish steaks. Maggie was not fazed in the least. She loved steak, and in her thirties after we arrived in Canada, she would often order a 12- or even 16-ounce steak in a restaurant. A favourite dining spot back then was Barberian's Steak House on Elm Street, where Maggie would usually tuck into either a thick rib eye or a generous portion of prime rib beef.

But let's get back to the ALTA two-steak blowout. I sat to one side and chowed down quietly, while Maggie fell behind in her meal. She fell behind because so many people wanted to talk to her.

At another ALTA meeting, one I didn't attend, Maggie and a group of technicians had gone to the aquarium in West Edmonton Mall. After the visit, they were sitting having a drink or four and discussing a "significant sighting". The "sighting" involved a whale at the aquarium. The whale had an erection "and it was THIS LONG". A full analysis followed, naturally, and there was the expected degree of laughing, chuckling, and snorting. Then a couple of older ladies came to their table and said how pleased they were to see a group of young women really enjoying themselves. Under further questioning, Maggie and her group explained who they were and what they had been laughing about. But they all went quiet on learning that these two ladies were trustees on the local public library board. The two older ladies must have been reasonably worldly and not easy to offend because they both smiled and told the younger women to "carry on".

The volunteer activity that I think Maggie got the greatest pleasure from was her role in helping operate the international business centre at the Royal Agricultural Winter Fair. The "Royal" is one of the largest shows of its kind in the world. Each year, it is attended by people involved in agriculture at all levels, from dozens of countries. The purpose of the international business centre is to provide a place where these people can go if they want a quiet space to make telephone calls or if they might need help in any aspect of their visit to the fair or to Toronto. Maggie's role in the operation of the international business centre had never been clearly defined, but without worrying about that at all, she just set about doing whatever needed to be done. There were attendance badges that needed to be made up and handed out. Glitches experienced by exhibitors and visitors needed to be dealt with. And there was the general business of greeting foreign guests and making them feel at home, something that came naturally to Maggie. I attended the Royal quite a few years to help at the business centre however I could.

The international centre was also a kind of hospitality suite. Bottled water was available, and supplies of it had to be retrieved from storage and brought to the centre on dollies to keep the coolers stocked. Small containers of chocolate milk were also available, and the same delivery and stocking requirements applied. The Royal always took place during a roughly two-week period in October-November, and fresh Ontario apples were available in large quantities. There were also cookies of various sorts, and Maggie and I enjoyed touring around in springtime each year sourcing those cookies.

Although the work at the business centre was steady and often taxing, there was a good deal of laughter. One incident in particular made the rounds. Maggie had noticed that a large puddle of water appeared regularly just outside the entrance to the business centre. Besides being concerned about it as a slip-and-fall hazard, Maggie could not see what had caused this puddle to be there. The riddle was resolved when she noticed one of the maintenance crew watering the flowers in a large pot to one side of the entrance. Not usually a problem, except that those flowers were artificial.

Maggie met many people from Europe and elsewhere at the Royal, and she remained in touch with some of them. One delightful gentleman, Richard, from the exquisite town of Malvern visited us regularly in our condo whenever he attended the Royal. Although a resident of Malvern, he comes from Yorkshire, something that is evident when one hears him speak. He and Maggie became close friends, despite backgrounds that were almost completely disparate. Richard admitted to weeping freely on learning of Maggie's death.

During one of his visits, Richard showed us how to make his trademark drink, concocted from gin and ginger beer.

"You start with an ounce of gin", he began.

"What? Just an ounce?" I objected in mock incredulity.

"Well, it's a Yorkshire ounce!"

He then began to make us drinks. He measured the ounce of gin, then added an ounce of ginger beer. Maggie and I thought it looked like a pretty small drink. Richard must have noted our disappointment.

"If it's too strong", he said, "you can dilute it by adding more gin."

It was clear that Richard's definition of "dilute" would not be confirmed by the *Oxford Dictionary*.

Each year at the Royal, Maggie would take time from the international business centre to go out into the main display area to tour the exhibits. There is always a large food hall, and one could locate some interesting offerings. Part of this food hall is always dedicated to foods from Northern Ontario. Every year, Maggie or I or both of us would cruise the Northern Ontario area. I often came away with cheese from Thornloe or from Kapuskasing or from wherever else was displaying their products. Maggie located the counter of frozen fish brought down from Manitoulin Island by Purvis Fisheries. This included smoked lake trout and smoked whitefish, things that were excellent on their own but were also fully suitable substitutes in kedgeree or Finnan haddie if Scottish smoked haddock wasn't available. Maggie would bring home several pieces of frozen fish bought during the early days of the show, but then load up near the end of the show when Mr. Purvis wanted to sell all the remaining fish he had trucked down to Toronto. There was also a company that sold pickerel from Lake of the Woods, and Maggie bought supplies of that because it was so delicious. Maggie became well known in the Northern Ontario area, in part because she had met some of the people during her COEF days but mostly because she would introduce herself, flash her fantastic smile, and they would be hooked.

In this and in previous chapters, I have provided the barest sketch of Maggie's working life, a life which was a dream of achievement. Maggie's success in her profession and in her many different jobs was powered by her unfailing interest in people of all sorts, her eagerness to help anyone in whatever ways she could, her great artesian well of enthusiasm, her ready beaming smile and immense human appeal, her matchless technical capabilities, and her unending curiosity about almost everything.

It was a privilege for me to take part in Maggie's career, even as just a bit player, or most often as someone on the sidelines. I can't describe my feelings of pride and love whenever I heard Maggie's many friends and colleagues, on many occasions, talk about how much she meant to them.

Maggie inspired so many people.

And Maggie certainly always inspired me.

CHAPTER 14

IMAGES OF MAGGIE

Many people have enduring images of Maggie: who she was, what she was like, things that stand out in their minds. Some statements reflecting these images appear throughout this book. What I want to do here is talk about a few of the things that evoke the clearest and most powerful images of Maggie for me.

MAGGIE'S SMILE

When Maggie smiled, her whole face lit up. And her smile and beaming face could light up a room and did so on many occasions.

Maggie's face retained a youthful quality throughout her life, and the pictures in this book capture that quality as it appeared through the years. Maggie's smile captivated me. I can see it still, and although it is one of the aspects of Maggie that I miss most, it is also something joyous that carries me forward.

MUSIC

Music was something that Maggie appreciated throughout her life. Her father, John, was a member of the Three Choirs, a group consisting of combined choirs from three cathedral cities: Gloucester, Worcester, and Hereford. Maggie attended many of the events in these cathedrals where her father sang, and I attended several after I came on the scene. The combination of music and cathedrals was something that affected Maggie, and as I watched her during any of these cathedral performances, I could see how deeply she was affected, both by the music and by the setting.

During the time I lived in Salisbury, almost a year, Maggie came down from London on numerous occasions, and if there was any musical performance in the cathedral, we would attend it. While we lived in London, we went through a Gilbert and Sullivan period, and we saw pretty much all their operettas as performed by the incomparable D'Oyly Carte company. Gilbert and Sullivan's music was so well known in England then (it seems now to have faded somewhat) that it was a pleasure to see others in the audience following along on their own copies of sheet music. The words and the music both invited performance of the pieces to be hammed liberally, and the D'Oyly Carte company were accommodating on this but without sacrificing the quality of the music itself.

There was often music in Maggie's home in Stroud, the music being generated by her father singing and accompanying himself on the piano, sometimes Maggie's brother, Chris, playing the violin, and anyone else joining in. Often, we all sang. Guests would take part as well. Occasions like that — in the Walker family's small and snug sitting room, the fire glowing, the piano booming, and voices raised in melody that was sometimes uncertain — these were moments of great human warmth.

In London, Maggie and I had a cheap record player and a few vinyl discs. Something that stands out in my mind was Maggie's version of the first line of the Mamas & the Papas' rendition of the song "My Girl", and she would always sing it and drown out what came from the record player:

"I've got sunshine on a flowery day."

Maggie also was fond of Benjamin Britten's work, particularly his *Ceremony of Carols*, which we listened to every year at Christmas time. Handel's *Messiah* was a piece that Maggie loved. Every year, for quite a few years in Toronto, we bought tickets to the *Messiah* performed by the Toronto Symphony and the Toronto Mendelssohn Choir. I can recall many occasions when we were listening to elements of the *Messiah*, and I would glance across at Maggie and see her looking rapt, having the appearance of a transfixed young girl.

We attended several performances of The King's Singers in Toronto, and the beauty of some of their music had Maggie on the edge of her seat. One particularly interesting performance involved The King's Singers, the Toronto Symphony, and Andrew Davis doing part of the story of *The Wind in the Willows* set to music. Maggie was thrilled at Andrew Davis's performance of Pan, a section of *The Wind in the Willows* that Maggie truly loved.

ENGLAND

England was a place that Maggie loved in many dimensions. It was clear to me during the summer we worked together at Harwell that the location held great meaning for her. The Ridgeway was not far from the Harwell site. The history of the place as a wartime RAF base was still evident then in some of the structures. Maggie talked about burial mounds, Wayland Smithy's cave, and wispy ends of tales about King Alfred and Arthur. The place seemed to be steeped in myth and legend.

Not only did Maggie and I meet at Harwell, it was also where Maggie's parents had met, and where she spent the first years of her childhood. Maggie had connections to another nuclear research site, Winfrith at Winfrith Newburgh in Dorset, but the connections were through friends and colleagues of her parents, people she knew as a child and who had worked at Harwell then moved to Winfrith. The Winfrith site for some years has been a place where no further nuclear research is done. But on one trip to England, when we were staying at a delightful B&B near Lulworth, Maggie asked if we could drive to the Winfrith site and take a look. We did. There was really nothing there to see. All the buildings had been emptied and demolished and the place was on its way back to a greenfield site. We stood at the gate, and Maggie gazed in for a few minutes, lost in her own thoughts. The elements that had made it a research site were gone, and the colleagues of her parents were gone as well. But it had been a real and meaningful part of her life.

The strongest memories I have of Maggie's connection to a location in England derive from my many visits, while we lived in London, to her family's home in Stroud. As an English country cottage, Sandpipers, Maggie's family home, was a highly memorable place, at one time being three eighteenth-century farm workers' cottages. Maggie often accompanied her mother on a tour of the garden to do weeding and occasionally to plant a cutting that her mother had "liberated" from the gardens of some stately home she had visited. The garden at Sandpipers consisted of a lush floral border along one side of a rectangular stretch of lawn, a rock garden on the opposite side, and a herb garden near the kitchen door. A large vegetable garden climbed the hill behind the rock garden. The floral border, the rock garden, and the herb garden were Joan's domain, while John looked after the lawn and the vegetable garden. There was something happening in these gardens in every season.

There were also walks to be taken on every visit I made to Stroud, generally up the lane from the front gate, into the wood that covered the top of the hill behind Sandpipers, then continuing across the field beyond the wood to a vantage point where one could gaze for miles across the lovely Severn Valley. The wood on top of the hill was a small larch copse consisting of several hundred trees, and it was one of my jobs to bring fallen larch branches down from this wood as kindling for the sitting-room fire. In spring when I was collecting this larch wood, I would often be accompanied by an English robin, nothing like the robins in Canada, but a much smaller bird that seems to enjoy accompanying people. These robins would often sit on branches less than five feet from me, watching companionably while I collected fallen wood. This larch wood has a local name, a name that appears on official and unofficial maps — the Fuzzes. Some of Maggie's ashes are scattered in the Fuzzes, so in some sense, Maggie and England have been reunited.

CATS

During one of my earliest visits to Sandpipers, I was introduced to a cat called Daisy. She was formally Maggie's cat, although Maggie's parents looked after her, Maggie seeing Daisy only during weekend trips home from London. Daisy was more than just a nominal pet, although she was that in reality. Maggie had always loved cats. A precursor to Daisy was Shell, a cat I never did meet. Contemporaries of Daisy were two cats called Pluto and Dido, named after the two research reactors at Harwell. Another cat in the Walker household, but at a different time, was named Iolanthe, another Gilbert and Sullivan reference, thus named, apparently, so that Joan could utter the musical call "Io-laan-the" from the back door.

When Maggie and I came to Canada, we very soon acquired three cats. A young cat called Rembrandt, kept by one of my aunts, had an unhappy kittenhood because he was chased and beaten by a second and older cat of my aunt, a cat called Tiger. Tiger was a vicious and bad-tempered little sod, and Maggie soon convinced my aunt to give Rembrandt to us. Rembrandt was a large male tabby, gentle as a lamb, very loving, and Maggie fell for him immediately. He was soon joined by a second cat, a pale tan-coloured male who evidently had somehow escaped an attempt to drown him, judging from his great fear of any kind of bag. We called this second cat Rubens, to follow an artistic theme. Rembrandt and Rubens became the best of friends. A third cat came along a couple of months later. This was a black cat with a few white markings who we called van Eyck; she was one of a family of kittens we found under our cottage in Hastings. I took this family of kittens to the humane society in Peterborough, since they had no future at our cottage except to become feral cats, but I brought one of the kittens, van Eyck, back to Toronto. These three cats, Rembrandt, Rubens, and van Eyck, went with us to Vienna in 1978. Although "van Eyck" was her official name, she was always called Squeaky because of her unique way of greeting us and demanding food.

We had two other batches of cats: Lois and Edward, and our current cats, Miles and Petula. Lois and Edward were named after people from the local music industry: Lois Marshall and nineteenth-century singer Edward Johnson, after whom a building in the Faculty of Music at the University of Toronto is named. There were three members in the third batch of cats, Miles, Petula, and Dusty. These three cats all came from the Toronto Humane Society as kittens from separate litters, all at the age of about five weeks. They were named after singers Miles Davis, Petula Clark, and Dusty Springfield, Miles being given his name because he is a black cat. Dusty died of liver cancer in 2017.

Maggie loved each of our cats deeply, and each in a specific and separate way.

Poetry and Literature

Maggie's taste in poetry and literature seemed to reflect her complexity as a person.

She was fond of nonsense verse, and she was happy to read or recite "Jabberwocky" or "The Walrus and the Carpenter" at any time. The songs of Flanders and Swann and of Tom Lehrer were well known by Maggie and her parents, and it was common to hear snippets from them quoted in a conversation, serious or otherwise. The hilarious novels by Michael Bond, featuring Monsieur Pamplemousse, were read avidly by both Maggie and me as they appeared. Maggie and I also very much enjoyed the spy stories of Anthony Price, and most recently she would dive into the strange, intriguing, complex, literate, and very enjoyable books by Jasper Fforde.

Maggie enjoyed reading and rereading Jane Austen, but her favourite historical fiction author was Georgette Heyer, and she read Heyer's novels many times. Maggie also enjoyed novels set in a bygone or imaginary time, books that tended to evoke nostalgia. She loved *The Wind in the Willows*. She also enjoyed books like *The Railway Children*, *Swallows and Amazons*, *The Water Babies*, *Just So Stories*, and *Children of the New Forest*.

I know that Maggie read *Cider With Rosie* by Laurie Lee. This is almost "must read" material for anyone raised in Stroud, since Laurie Lee was born and raised in the village of Slad, just a couple of kilometres from Sandpipers. *Cider With Rosie* is both a coming-of-age story and a tale of the passing of an entire era. The writing is exquisite, but I don't have a clear picture of what Maggie thought of the book since she and I never did discuss it. What she thought of it might well have depended on how old she was when she chose, or was told, to read it.

Maggie did not enjoy having things read to her. She always wanted reading to be a private pleasure. She was also not fond of group discussions of poetry or novels, and that explains her reluctance ever to join a book club. There were poems that I know she liked. One that she had learned as a preteen she came back to again and again. It captured for Maggie a complex mixture of recollections of youth, an appreciation of rural beauty, a sort of timelessness, and a certain innocent view of religion. That poem was "The Oxen" by Thomas Hardy, not a complex or sophisticated poem, but I will always associate it with Maggie. As with a good deal of Hardy's writing, "The Oxen" draws its strength from a rural setting and expresses great yearning.

Religion

Discussion was almost a staple of life in Maggie's family, and it was easy for discussion to become heated and turn into arguments, and the arguments sometimes became serious enough that gauntlets were thrown down.

This family penchant for vigorous discussion was not appreciated in all quarters. Maggie recalled, with some pride, that one of her instructors in a class called Religious Knowledge, accused Maggie of being dogmatic, apparently not recognizing the irony. Maggie loved visiting churches and cathedrals, and although she did not attend services in any church, she was, in a very real sense, religious. It was just that her sense of religion was not linked strongly to any conventional church.

Maggie always said that her parents were atheists, although I wasn't convinced of that. But Maggie knew her parents far longer, and in a different way than I did, so I never questioned her view on that matter. I never did discuss religion with either Joan or John, and although neither of them attended a church, John sang religious music regularly as part of his involvement in the Three Choirs, and I know that they both felt that the church was an important cohesive element of society's overall context. Maggie and I never discussed religion seriously, and I know that was an omission on my part.

Politics

Maggie admired and respected her mother, Joan, who was an impressive raw intellect. Joan and John both professed to be conservative, both in philosophical outlook and politically. John was born in York and raised in the seaside town of Scarborough, and his conversation sometimes betrayed, at least to me, a socialist or socialist-leaning tinge, something that one might expect from someone raised at that time and in that part of England. Joan was born in Bristol and raised in a household where her father was a housebuilder, and so lived by his wits and the sweat of his brow. In what came closest to a discussion of politics, but really wasn't, John said to me one time, when I asked him why he had joined the Conservative Club in Stroud, that one could get the best gin and tonics there.

Maggie tended to favour the Conservatives in Canada, although she was shortchanged by the ridiculous requirement at all levels to be a Canadian citizen in order to be able to vote. (When I lived in London, I was not a UK citizen but was able to vote in every election.) Maggie stopped short of taking out Canadian citizenship for complex emotional reasons, and I never questioned or disputed her view on that. It was her choice entirely. During the years of Stephen Harper, Maggie was a supporter initially, but she gradually soured on Harper and his rather extreme views on a number of matters.

Maggie asked me on several occasions about my political views, and I always got the sense that my answers weren't adequate for her. My answer was that I thought politicians should be fiscally conservative but socially liberal, since one needed the former in order to be able to pay for the latter, and social conservatism in Canada always seemed to me to lead to some kind of extremism. So politics was an area that Maggie and I didn't talk about much.

MY IMAGES

The complexity that was Maggie always was and remains part of the reason why I was so strongly attracted to her. Throughout our life together, it was often the case that I didn't know quite what was going to happen next, was uncertain about the source and intensity of the current Maggie enthusiasm (not to mention the next one), and often would find myself suddenly overwhelmed just to be in Maggie's presence. To say that these things added spice to our life presents a pale image of the reality.

In the end, I keep coming back to Maggie's smile. It reflects for me everything that has always meant so much: her delight in so many things, her uniformly positive outlook on people and the world, her desire for friendship and connection, her wellspring of curiosity that could engage with the world at any time, her clear-sightedness and often intense focus, the many pleasures she enjoyed so fully, and her generous capacity for love. Maggie's smile always reminded me — and continues to remind me — of her commitment to our joint life together, despite bumps along the way.

I miss Maggie. I know I will always miss her. But what I gained from our life together glows brilliantly.

CHAPTER 15

ACCOMPLISHMENT —
WHAT MAGGIE ACHIEVED

How does one sum up a person?

I think it's an impossible task if what one wants is an all-inclusive and definitive statement. Each of us is a complex amalgam deriving from many sources: genetics, the great pool of home and family influences, urban or rural backdrops, education at all levels, friendships, good and bad experiences with others, preferences each of us is born with and develops in early life, cultural background, the standards each of us defines for ourselves and applies to what we do, how we behave and react to situations, how we judge others, and the various opportunities that come our way and that we grasp or let pass.

Each of us comes to develop some internal image of herself or himself as we mature, but we also learn that any individual cannot reliably view themselves impartially, that others often do a better job of that, but that accepting any judgment of who and what we are — a judgment by ourselves or by others — is something that must be done with care and not uncritically.

Having known Maggie for fifty-two years, I was the person closest to her. But even that was no guarantee that I "knew" her in all her complexity. Maggie regularly surprised, delighted, and fascinated me. I sometimes misunderstood Maggie. I sometimes disagreed with her, too often I think and mostly due to my own failings. The surprise, delight, and fascination that Maggie delivered to me was closely entwined with my love for her, and that love was constantly being renewed. All these things were based on the person I knew as Maggie, but I think that, to a great extent, they arose because of the Maggie I kept getting to know throughout our lives together. It was the unknown Maggie, the unexpected Maggie, the Maggie who was continuously being discovered — these were important sources of the ongoing charm and challenge of living with her.

But in the end, there is some reality that does need to be summarized. I can try to do this in three ways.

Maggie and her work

In her working life, Maggie took advantage of every aspect of her wide experience. In the end she was able to marshal a stunning range of capabilities and competences. Some of these were her knowledge of people, her understanding of all aspects — positive and negative — of the business and commercial world, her command of a surprisingly wide range of specialist topics, the apparently effortless use of her wide-ranging but finely developed sense of humour, and her ease at being able to relate to people through seminars, presentations, courses, and informal discussions. This made her a highly valued colleague and contractor and working in this medium was something she loved. For me, to see Maggie at work and to see how her work animated her was a privilege.

Maggie as my Beatrice

As I see things, the most personal and focussed area of reality that Maggie applied herself to was our relationship, hers and mine. Much of it was a private domain that was constructed in important ways through her efforts. It was a rich blend of humour, cultural elements, cerebral pursuits, culinary delight, a fertile imagination for elements of decoration of all sorts, endless curiosity about everything, her large contribution to our shared social approach to the world, a vast field of quirkiness, and in general, all the components of the powerful glue that bonded us to each other. Although this was an area limited in extent compared to the rest of Maggie's world, she poured enormous effort into it, and I acknowledge being the sole and eternally grateful benefactor.

MAGGIE'S LEGACY

The most important impact Maggie had on the world is what she leaves in the minds and hearts of the people who knew her.

My family were all won over by her immediately. This was despite the large social and cultural differences that separated Maggie's immediate family in England and my immediate family in Canada. Maggie won people over simply through immense personal charm.

Through Maggie's work and my work, we met people all over the world, and the regard those people had for Maggie was indicated by the volume of mail, dripping love and loss, that I received after her death. Maggie had colleagues across North America and Europe who loved her dearly for who she was. There are friends in Britain and Europe who remained in close touch with Maggie over decades, a few of them dating from a time before my entry onto the scene. I've lost count of the number of friends Maggie had in Toronto and nearby areas.

I know many people who Maggie inspired. And the regard and love Maggie's many friends and colleagues shared with her made Maggie's life that much richer.

There is another aspect of Maggie's legacy, and that is the traces she left in me, something that was built up during more than fifty years of intimate connection. I don't want to give the impression that Maggie and I had a marriage that was somehow "perfect". To me it was an exceptional marriage. It was a marriage full of love. Both of us being strong minded, we had disagreements and occasionally there was strife, but that's normal.

Nor am I trying to say that our marriage was unique. There are plenty of successful marriages out there. And there are many individuals, like Maggie, who others would not hesitate to claim as friends. They are people any country would be proud to call citizens.

I undertook to write this book because Maggie had those qualities. She influenced my life powerfully and I wanted to offer a tribute to her — this book.

My life with Maggie was rich, fulfilling, exciting, and more than I feel I deserved. My cup really did run over in the sense that my life with Maggie delivered a quotient of laughter, loving, and learning that leaves me speechless when I look back on it. I hope, and I believe, that Maggie's cup was equally over-filled. Our shared life, Maggie's and mine, forged a large set of bright and lasting images.

There is something here that needs extra emphasis. It is pretty much impossible for me to overstate the impact that Maggie's presence had on the course of my life and on who I became. In speaking to friends and family, I have found it difficult to get across just how deeply my worldview changed between the ages of about eighteen and thirty-five. My first visit to Europe left me overwhelmed, and to some extent I suppose that I was a tabula rasa, or using another metaphor, a fruit ripe to be picked. But subsequent events could have unfolded otherwise. I could have followed a path that did not involve Maggie. My life could have been very different in that case. My web of human connections might have been less challenging and not as rich. I might not have been immersed in an Old World culture, and that would have been my loss. It was the bond I formed with Maggie, and the resulting long-term commitment to such an extraordinary person that resulted in me acquiring a deeper, wider, stronger, richer, and permanently altered view of the world. I have been at pains throughout this book to describe that change and how momentous Maggie's effect was on my life, both as a result of our shared journey through the world and Maggie's direct influence on me as an individual. Maggie's impact on me — emotionally, intellectually, culturally, and practically — was nothing short of life-changing.

I am left now with a great loss. But far outweighing that loss is the life's treasure that Maggie has handed off to me. That treasure comes from many sources. There is now in my memory what often seems an endless stream of vivid images from my life with Maggie as a woman, a lover, a wife, a friend, a partner, a soulmate, and a seeker of lovely pebbles on a great beach. There is the music and books we enjoyed. There is the food and wine we savoured. There are memories of people and places from our extensive travels. There are my connections to

Maggie's family. There is the reflected love from Maggie's friends. There are physical reminders that now surround me on all sides and are imbued with Maggie's curiosity, whimsy, sense of value, and the love of a lifetime together.

I continue to give thanks and will do so as long as I am able for the many images that remain with me — of a brilliant smile, of ideas, of laughter, of adventure, of learning, of a soft voice, of compassion, of friends' company embraced, of a singsong welcome, of beautiful moments shared, and of the gentle touch of loving fingers and lips.

THE MANY FACES OF MAGGIE

A selection of thirty-two pictures completes this book. The pictures cover almost all of Maggie's life. And what a life it was!

MAGGIE'S SMILE WAS ALWAYS THERE

MAGGIE AND CHRIS IN THE 1950S

MAGGIE AND CHRIS, YOUNG ADOLESCENTS

YOUNG MAGGIE AND CHRIS IN STROUD

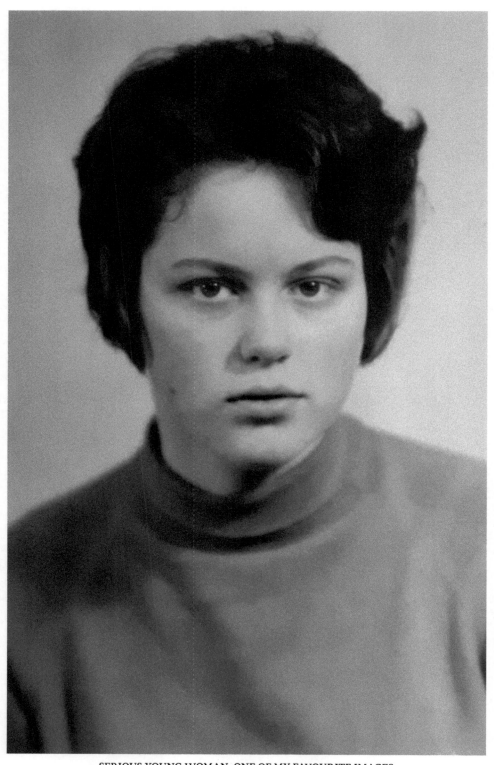

SERIOUS YOUNG WOMAN, ONE OF MY FAVOURITE IMAGES

ASPIRING MODEL IN LONDON, 1972

**BRIDESMAID AT
DENYSE AND CHRIS'S WEDDING, 1972**

IN TORONTO, 1976

INSPECTING GORGE NEAR GRASKOP EASTERN TRANSVAAL, EASTER 1980

ON HONEYMOON IN BRITISH COLUMBIA

NOT QUITE BOHEMIAN

MAGGIE OVERSEEING LAYOUT OF UNCITRAL LIBRARY, VIENNA

PART OF THE COMPLETED UNCITRAL LIBRARY

SOME UNCITRAL STAFF (MAGGIE EXTREME LEFT, UNCITRAL DIRECTOR THIRD FROM LEFT)

YOUTHFUL HAPPY TIMES

PLAYING IN THE SAND, CALIFORNIA 1980S

PLAYING IN THE WATER, CALIFORNIA 1980S

HAPPY TIMES WITH BROTHER CHRIS

HAMMING IT UP

MAGGIE AND SISTER-IN-LAW DENYSE

IN PIONEER GARB, SHERBROOKE, NOVA SCOTIA

IN MARKET AT AIX-EN-PROVENCE

EXPLORING VINON, PROVENCE

MIDDAY SHADE

RELAXING IN ST PAUL LEZ DURANCE

MAGGIE WITH HEDGEHOG

ENJOYING THE NOVA SCOTIA SHORE

MAGGIE WITH GREAT NIECE

MAGGIE IN PARTY MODE

MAGGIE ENJOYING PRIVATE JOKE

MAGGIE ON THE HOTHOUSE PATIO

THE INFECTIOUS SMILE, MAGGIE IN THE MID-1980S

ACKNOWLEDGEMENTS

My thanks to Chris Walker, Maggie's twin brother and my brother-in-law, for his assistance on family details and photos. Chris now seems more like a brother than a brother-in-law.

My thanks to John Lockett, Maggie's and my long-time friend, for information associated with the atomic energy research site at Harwell.

Four of Maggie's close colleagues at various stages in her career have been generous with their time in reviewing text relating to Maggie's working life. Thank you, in alphabetical order, to Judy Dunn, Louise Grady, Ulla de Stricker, and Debbie Walker.

My thanks to many residents of the Market Square condominium complex, where Maggie and I lived for ten years and where I continue to live, for their unfailing support in so many ways. Good friends all.

My thanks to Victoria Feistner, a friend to both Maggie and me, for her work on the covers, layout, and photos in this book. Thanks, Victoria.

Clarisse Smith offered editorial comments that improved the text considerably, and she held her ground in discussions with someone decades her senior. Thanks, Clarisse.

It was a pleasure to work again with Paula Chiarcos, the copy editor for this book. Editor extraordinaire. Thanks, Paula.

A particular vote of thanks to my publisher, Greg Ioannou, of Iguana Books, for his ongoing belief in my writing and his generous support for this book.

ABOUT THE AUTHOR

Keith Weaver comes from humble origins in central Ontario. Even as a pre-teen, however, he was aware of and interested in the wider world both past and present, and through this interest it became clear to him by the age of fifteen that he would do everything he could to embrace that wider world. That this interest would lead him to Europe, to Maggie, and to a very rich life was beyond imagining back then.

From his connection to Maggie that began in 1970, and after graduating from the University of Toronto in chemical engineering in 1971, he spent four years in London, after which he and Maggie came to Canada. Following a thirty-seven year engineering career, he retired and took up a long-time writing interest.

Keith Weaver has had ten books published, including this one. There are more to come. The first nine books all bear the stamp of Maggie's love of English and of good writing.

Keith lives in Toronto with two cats, a decent wine cellar, and too many books. He is an accomplished bread maker, loves cooking, is an addicted reader, enjoys languages, and is always trying to find more time to study philosophy and history.

OTHER TITLES BY THIS AUTHOR

An Uncompromising Place
Un Endroit Sans Compromis
The Recipe Cops
Balsam Sirens
Mr Drumlin's Orchard
Sicilian Refuge
Rolls
Walking With Albert and Other Stories
Fool's Cap and Other Stories